C A P S T O N E

work smarter

Smart books are the essential primers to the key issues facing business people. They are practical guides designed to give killer approaches to key business subjects, and deliver sound principles in a style that is both informative and has attitude. They are the perfect resource for time-starved business people everywhere!

The newest **Smart** titles are:

Smart **Leadership**	JONATHAN YUDELOWITZ
Smart **Marketing**	JOHN MARIOTTI
Smart **Finance**	KEN LANGDON
Smart **Strategy**	RICHARD KOCH
Smart **Business**	JAMES LEIBERT
Smart **Risk**	ANDREW HOLMES

Also available in the Smart series:

Smart Things to Know About **Brands and Branding**	JOHN MARIOTTI
Smart Things to Know About **Change**	DAVID FIRTH
Smart Things to Know About **Consultancy**	PATRICK FORSYTH
Smart Things to Know About **CRM**	DAVID HARVEY
Smart Things to Know About **Culture**	DONNA DEEPROSE
Smart Things to Know About **Customers**	ROS JAY
Smart Things to Know About **Decision Making**	KEN LANGDON
Smart Things to Know About **E-commerce**	MIKE CUNNINGHAM
Smart Things to Know About **Growth**	TONY GRUNDY
Smart Things to Know About **Innovation and Creativity**	DENNIS SHERWOOD
Smart Things to Know About **Knowledge Management**	THOMAS KOULOPOULOS
Smart Things to Know About **Lifelong Learning**	ANDREW HOLMES
Smart Things to Know About **Managing Projects**	DONNA DEEPROSE
Smart Things to Know About **Mergers & Acquisitions**	TONY GRUNDY
Smart Things to Know About **Motivation**	DONNA DEEPROSE
Smart Things to Know About **Partnerships**	JOHN MARIOTTI
Smart Things to Know About **People Management**	DAVID FIRTH
Smart Things to Know About **Scenario Planning**	TONY KIPPENBERGER
Smart Things to Know About **Six Sigma**	ANDREW BERGER
Smart Things to Know About **Managing Talent**	STEPHANIE OVERMAN
Smart Things to Know About **Teams**	ANNEMARIE CARRACIOLO
Smart Things to Know About **Technology Management**	ANDREW HOLMES
Smart Things to Know About **Your Career**	JOHN MIDDLETON

smart

•➔ risk

ANDREW HOLMES

The right of Andrew Holmes to be identified as the author of this book has been asserted in accordance with the Copyright, Designs and Patents Act 1988

First published 2004 by
Capstone Publishing Limited (A Wiley Company)
The Atrium
Southern Gate
Chichester
West Sussex PO19 8SQ
http://www.wileyeurope.com

CIP catalogue records for this book are available from the British Library and the US Library of Congress

ISBN 1-84112-507-5

Typeset in Meridien 10/14pt by Sparks Computer Solutions Ltd
http://www.sparks.co.uk

Printed and bound by TJ International Ltd, Padstow, Cornwall

10 9 8 7 6 5 4 3 2 1

Contents

Introduction:
You Can't Escape Risk

Smart quotes

Companies around the world have been taking a fresh, hard look at managing risk. In the process, they are redefining the role of risk management in achieving objectives, and ultimately, increasing shareholder value. Their main goal is not to eliminate risk, but rather to be proactive in assessing and managing risk for their own advantage.

PricewaterhouseCoopers

None of us can escape risk. It is all around us. And over the last few years we have become more sensitive and perhaps a little more accustomed to the types of risk that we face. For example, the Y2K bug highlighted the risks of an overdependence on computer-based technology; the terrorist attacks on the Twin Towers in New York reinforced the risks associated with a dissatisfaction with the growing power and dominance of the US and Western capitalism; and the economic turbulence following the demise of the dotcom investment bubble brought into sharp relief the major risks we face when economies struggle to grow. There is also a growing recognition that risk is more complex and systemic than it has ever been. Indeed, Tony Blair, the UK's Prime Minister, has publicly stated that the complex nature of risk is making it much harder to identify, manage and control and his

2003 New Year message was particularly negative and focused on risk. Blair's statement comes in the wake of the continued threats of terrorist attacks, which themselves tend to heighten everyone's awareness of the larger, but perhaps more remote, risks we have to deal with and often feel that we can't.

Smart quotes

Risk management has become elevated because society is more worried about the downside of risk, and managers are worried about appearing to be reckless and irresponsible in running an operation. Managers feel that, if a mistake were to happen, they would be unable to put their side of the story. Better to be safe than sorry. Senior managers therefore have new demands today – demands for information and assurances about risk. As a result, corporations have overseen an unprecedented number of initiatives under the risk management umbrella.

Benjamin Hunt

For example, in January 2003, police foiled a gang that was manufacturing ricin for an attack in London. Although deadly when you come into contact with it, the likelihood of any one of us being killed in such an attack is very remote. But, once we are aware of the potential threat we all tend to believe that we are exposed to a much greater risk than we realize. In a similar vein, the risks of a warmer world, and of pollution in general, are making individuals – and businesses in particular – more concerned about pollution and the impacts of our carelessness when it comes to the environment.

However well organised the foundations of life might be, life must always be full of risks.

Havelock Ellis

Despite this increased sensitivity and awareness of risk, we tend to be poor at assessing and managing those risks that we have direct control over. In general we have a very poor understanding of the mathematical foundations that underlie effective risk management. And at the heart of this ignorance lies our inability to grasp the concept of probability. So, although a terrorist attack on central London is probable, it is far more remote than being run over by a car. But we tend to believe the opposite. As a result we tend to pass through our daily lives managing the most common risks intuitively rather than explicitly. We all know that walking across the road has an inherent risk associated with it, as does driving a car, air travel and, increasingly in the UK, rail travel. As these and similar risks are still quite remote, we don't tend to give them much thought until someone we know or love is involved in an incident such as a car crash. Compare this to the much higher danger we associate with a terrorist attack, which is much less likely to happen.

To a lesser or greater extent, we are taught from an early age to be careful and manage the low-level risks we face quite carefully (such as crossing the road) or dismissing them to fate (as in air travel). So unless we are doing something that departs significantly from our daily routine, such as jumping out of a plane or scuba diving, for example, we tend to take risk for granted and we often don't give it a second's thought. Also, at the individual level, if we take a risk and fail to manage it properly, the damage is limited to us, and maybe our near relatives. In other words, few people are affected. However, when we elevate risk to the corporate or national levels we can see more complex factors at work. For example, the BSE and foot-and-mouth crises in the UK resulted in many people's livelihoods being virtually destroyed in the wake of a massive drop in livestock values in the former, and the near complete shutdown of the countryside during the latter. The foot-and-mouth crisis not only affected the farming communities, but also those involved with the tourist industry. The key thing to remember about risk is that its effects are rarely isolated. Similarly, an entire country can be put at risk when its economy is managed badly. It is no surprise that there are numerous examples of countries having to be bailed out by the International Monetary Fund.

Smart quotes

The September 11th attacks underlined what a complex, risky world we live in; a world in which borders are open, communications are cheap, information plentiful, knowledge easy to acquire and as a result risks and threats come from unusual sources.

Charles Leadbeater

The management of risk tends to be focused on the organization, as this is where the major complexities exist. This is because the implications of poor risk management can have significant impacts on a wider number of stakeholders including shareholders and employees, as well as the national and local economies. It is also because the nature of risk within organizations is far more complex than the simple risks we have to manage as individuals. Such risks cover the strategic and financial aspects of the business, as well as those associated with maintaining effective operations and delivering change through projects and programmes.

Where there is risk, there is opportunity.

Managing risk is therefore an essential skill of all modern corporations. And, for those who manage risk well, the rewards can be great. For example, Tesco, the giant UK food retailer, has consistently led the competition by being the first to market with new innovations such as loyalty cards and Internet grocery shopping. Being first to market offers great first-mover opportunity, but it also involves the careful management of risk. It is clear that Tesco's foray into the Internet shopping arena was not without its problems as, early on, the technology was not as robust as it needed to be and the system was principally based on faxes being sent to stores for order fulfilment. However, through ongoing improvements, Tesco's Internet shopping offering has gone from strength to strength and has captured the market. It now has over 1 million registered customers and processes 70,000 orders a week. The system has recently been adopted by the US company Safeway and is a role model of Internet grocery shopping. Its success is down to learning from earlier failures, focusing on in-store pickers rather than relying on warehouse facilities, its simplicity and Tesco's ability to manage risk.

BP

In August 2001 BP's second-quarter profits came in at a record $7.9 billion, up 25 per cent on the previous year. Yet ten years ago, BP was almost bankrupt. The achievements of the current chief executive, Lord Browne, who has transformed the company, cannot be overstated. He achieved this turnaround by slashing costs, attacking overcapacity and taking risks by acquiring Amoco and Atlantic Richfield. These acquisitions were made at a time when oil prices were hovering around $10 per barrel and the oil industry was in a poor state of repair. Hindsight suggests he purchased the two rivals at a knockdown price, but what it points to is an astute management of risk.

Conversely, companies that fail to manage their risks, or that behave badly, can soon go out of business. The failures of Enron, WorldCom and, probably most importantly, the Big Five accountancy firm Andersen are shining examples of the impacts of risk, albeit in its extreme.

Take Enron, for example: before failing it was the darling of the stock markets and could not put a foot wrong. Then, when it went public, with the need to restate its accounts, it began to unravel. What makes the failure of Enron so significant was that it was the biggest in US corporate history. But it does not end there, as Enron employees were persuaded to sink their pension money into its shares which, according to the analysts and Enron executives, would only continue to rise. When they fell – precipitously – many employees literally lost everything. The executives naturally walked away with millions of dollars – until they were caught.

Taking financial and business risks such as those associated with Enron requires a large degree of collusion. The impacts of Enron and the scandals that followed did more damage to the global economy than the attack on the World Trade Center. In many ways, one of the most significant casualties arising from the Enron affair was Andersen which, up until then, had a solid reputation and a powerful brand. But, unlike a company that sells products, Andersen traded on trust. Once broken, it was impossible to retrieve, as client after client deserted it. Eventually the firm was broken up and sold off to its rivals. The demise of Andersen is a perfect example of brand risk.

Enron, WorldCom and Andersen demonstrate the dangers of poor risk management or when risks are allowed to fester beneath the corporate radar. However, these are extreme examples that serve as beacons to us all. The majority of organizations manage their risks more effectively and, usually, more openly. However, few can be considered world class.

It is clear so far that failing to manage risk can result in financial loss of one kind or another. As well as the examples cited above, others come to mind. For example, the failure of governments to manage their economies can lead to boom and bust, recessions and, in extreme cases, depressions. The depression that followed the Wall Street Crash in 1929

Bubbles, black holes and scandals

The scandals we have witnessed recently are, of course, nothing new, as there have been many in the past, often with equally devastating effects. However, reading down the list below suggests that they are occurring with greater frequency, which is somewhat worrying.

- 1637 – the bursting of the Tulip Bubble. When the market for tulips collapsed, the price of bulbs had risen 5900 per cent. Investors lost everything they owned.

- 1720 – the bursting of the South Sea Bubble. A company without any track record or assets was able to convince investors to sell their holdings in the worthless Pacific Territories at higher and higher prices. When the bubble eventually burst, it took over 100 years for the London Stock Market to recover.
- 1929 – Wall Street Crash.
- 1963 – salad oil scandal. American Express managed to lose an amount equivalent to its net value when it believed that financier Tony De Angelis had huge amounts of salad oil stored in New Jersey refineries when in fact he hadn't.
- 1979 – US businesses lose $1 billion as a result of the Iranian revolution and the overthrow of the Shah.
- 1991 – Bank of Credit and Commerce International is accused of illegally controlling a majority of stock in Washington's largest bank-holding company, First American Bankshares.
- 1994 – Kidder Peabody fiasco. Joseph Jett was accused of generating $350 million in phantom profits between 1991 and 1994.
- 1995 – Nick Leeson brought down Barings Bank after he managed to lose $1.3 billion on derivatives. The bank was later sold to ING for £1.
- 1996 – Sumitomo Copper scandal. A trader was accused of conducting unauthorized trades over ten years, losing $1.8 billion.
- 1997 – NatWest Markets discover a £50 million hole in its options trading book.
- 1998 – failure of the Long Term Capital Management Hedge fund that almost brought down the entire global finance system. At one point the exposure of the fund was in the region of £3 trillion.
- 2000 – bursting of the dotcom bubble wiped billions off share prices as it was realized that the New Economy was not that new at all. The global economy and businesses are only now in the tentative stages of recovery.
- 2001 – accounting scandals including Enron, Tyco and WorldCom rock the world finance system. The wave of corporate governance scandals that followed Enron has cost the US economy in the region of $35 billion – as much as a $10 per barrel rise in the price of oil.
- 2002 – Andersen: the global professional firm is broken up and sold to its rivals in the wake of the Enron scandal, which claimed the Andersen brand in a matter or months.

was in part caused by the actions of the central banks that raised interest rates in the hope of keeping money and gold from flowing out of their countries. This prolonged the economic gloom far longer than was really necessary. Similar errors of judgements in the UK during the 1970s led to the International Monetary Fund bailing out the then Labour administration. And, more recently, in 1998 we saw the Russian government default on their domestic debt and trigger panic in the emerging markets. But risk and risk management extend well beyond the pure financial risks that people and organizations tend to focus on. There are other types of risk, with different consequences, that also have to be managed. Admittedly, most have a financial consequence, but this often occurs once the risk has run its course.

At the strategic level, organizations can be seduced into rushing into investing in speculative bubbles and seeking first-mover advantage without thinking about the downside. Many also follow the herd and widen their operations beyond their core competencies in the pursuit of profit. The rush into Internet banking, for example, resulted in many financial institutions investing many millions in the hope of capturing market share. Only when they realized that there were too many banks chasing too few customers did they pull the plug. The same can be said of the technological bubble that burst with the failure of the Internet start-up businesses. This resulted in billions of market capitalization being wiped off the value of telecom and technology stocks overnight.

At the project and programme level, many hundreds of millions of dollars can be wasted on major construction projects, change initiatives and technology programmes without any benefit to the organization. For example, the Confirm travel reservation project that failed during the early 1990s cost its backers $125 million; in 1992 the failure of Westpac's CS90 project cost the company A$125; and the Department of Social Security's Operational Strategy cost the UK government £2.3 billion. With an increasing emphasis on projects and programmes to deliver strategic change, the impact of poor risk management can be disastrous.

Even at the personal level we are exposed to a multitude of low-level risks, many of which we are oblivious to, or just don't feel able (or willing) to manage. Many people find themselves spending beyond their means; others find their careers terminated at short notice; others still fail to look after their health and then develop fatal or near-fatal medical conditions. Risks affect us at every level, individually, corporately, nationally and globally. Thus, the ability to manage risk is a key skill that we all need, irrespective of our role or position in society.

Answer the following questions to see how on top of risk you are

Answer 0 = no; 5 = partially; 10 = yes

1   Do I know what the top ten risks facing the business are?
2   Do I know what my own attitude to risk is?
3   Do I know what my company's attitude to risk is?
4   Do I understand the significance of human behaviour in the reporting and management of risk?
5   Am I sufficiently familiar with the concepts of probability and statistics to understand what risk statements actually mean?
6   Can I get the information I need in relation to the risks in the business and how they are being managed?
7   Can I explain to others in my organization the types of risk that they are likely to face?
8   Am I able to assess my personal risks in their widest sense?
9   Does my organization have a risk culture, in which people are able to take/raise risks without retribution?
10   Does my company have risk management processes, roles and responsibilities in place and are these operating effectively?
11   Do I know what support is available to me in the management of risk?
12   Do I have access to tools to help keep my risk management knowledge and skills up to date?
13   Am I confident in senior management's ability to manage risk?

Smart risk management requires us to become more open and honest in the way we identify and manage risk. It also requires us to expand our understanding of risk management. This requires us to:

- understand what risk management is and why it matters, which has to include a rudimentary grasp of probability (Chapter 1);

- recognize the complete risk landscape by understanding the categories of risk that have to be managed (Chapter 2);

- know our risk appetite, as this defines the boundary between those risks we are willing to take and those we aren't (Chapter 3);

- formalize the risk management process (Chapter 4);

- develop a risk culture; everyone within the corporation should be able to raise and manage risk; many do not because their culture restricts them; a critical success factor is the generation and maintenance of a risk management culture (Chapter 5);

- learn from success and failure (Chapter 6);

- use risk tools and models to support decision making (Chapter 7); and

- recognize that risk management is closely linked to innovation, which in turn is vital for the long-term survival of the organization (Chapter 8).

This book reviews risk and risk management from a very wide perspective. It is designed to provide you with a broad base from which you can explore some of the areas in greater detail. So, rather than go into the minutiae of financial modelling, or environmental risk analysis, it will introduce the key topics and their impacts and provide you with all the smart thinking you need in order to take an active stance when

Smart answers to tough questions

Q. What is so important about risk management? What will it bring to my company and me?

A. Risk management is one of the most important processes within any organization and is crucial for future long-term success. Managing risks wisely by focusing on those that matter, creating a risk culture and applying effective processes ensures that you are in control of risk, not the other way around. Here are just some of the ...

Benefits for the smart individual
- Increased ability to deal with change.
- Better analysis of the opportunities that face you during your career.
- Enhanced awareness and understanding of the risks that you take and their consequences.
- Long-term survival in an increasingly competitive workplace.

Benefits for the smart organization
- Enhanced understanding of the risks that are facing the organization.
- Better understanding of how risks interact.
- Clearer view of the risks that have to be managed, monitored and controlled at all levels within the enterprise.
- Increased sensitivity to the implications of taking different courses of action.
- More effective assessment of the financial implications of investments, lending decisions and the markets.
- Development of a risk culture that involves viewing risks as opportunities, rather than threats.
- More visibility of the risks that the organization wishes to take deliberately as well as those it needs to guard against and actively avoid.
- Long-term survival in an increasingly competitive global economy.

it comes to risk and risk management. In addition, I have included some core techniques and tools and a glossary of key terms. At the end of the book, you should have a sound understanding of the nature of risk, be up to speed with some of the latest issues and thinking on risk management and have a clear idea of what risks you might need to be attending to. What this book will not give you is a risk-free future. I'm afraid life is far too complicated for that. And, in any case, it would never provide us with the flip side of risk – opportunity.

1 The Foundations of Risk Management

Smart quotes

The revolutionary idea that defines the boundary between modern times and the past is the mastery of risk.

Peter Bernstein

As we saw in the introduction, we face a multitude of risks in our daily lives and the number and complexity of these has grown, particularly over the last 50 years or so. Complexity is a major driver of risk because of its ability to distort our understanding and cloud our judgement. In some cases, it can make us feel like rabbits caught in the headlights of a speeding car – not knowing which way to turn. But despite such complexity, risk is a fundamental discipline within all businesses, irrespective of their market sector, size or composition.

In very simple terms, risk management involves following a deliberate set of actions designed to identify, quantify, manage and then monitor those things, events or actions that could lead to loss, which in most cases equates to financial loss. This implies that risk management is an active process requiring commitment and focus. But in many instances there is insufficient data about a risk to define it precisely, which makes the process more difficult and necessitates greater vigilance. As a result, great attempts have been, and continue to be, made at modelling and assessing risk, which in some cases have bordered on pseudo-science.

But irrespective of how precise the process is, it involves the application of judgement and requires the organization to make certain assumptions about the future. For example, although assessing the likelihood of a road accident is quite easy, assessing the risk of nuclear meltdown is very difficult. This is because in the case of road accidents there is plenty of information available against which the risk can be modelled but in the nuclear meltdown case there is very little. This separates risk (which can be managed) from uncertainty (which generally cannot be managed without the construction of theoretical models – because there is insufficient historical information on which to assess the risks). Therefore, in order to manage risks effectively it is necessary to categorize the types of risk that organizations are exposed to and then manage them accordingly. A classification of risk is discussed in greater detail in Chapter 2. This chapter outlines why risk management is important, describes its evolution and spends some time covering its central concept; probability.

Smart quotes

Risk management is about taking risks knowingly. An effective risk management structure allows an organization to understand the risks in any initiative and take informed decisions on whether and how the risks should be managed. Corporate governance and risk management is about how an organization can better understand its risk, to improve and deliver its objectives.

KPMG

Risk management matters. Put very starkly, companies cannot survive without some degree of risk management. Those that undertake projects, develop new products, seek to raise debt on the markets and trade globally all have to manage uncertainties and hence the risks that their ventures may fail. For those that undertake projects, there is no guarantee that they will succeed. For those that develop new products, they have to contend with the uncertainties of product failure and acceptance. For those that want to raise debt, they have to demonstrate good corporate governance in order to get the highest credit rating, which in turn means a lower interest rate. And finally, for those who trade globally, they have to deal with issues associated with currency variations, and the political and economic stability of their overseas hosts, as well as the activities of non-governmental organizations. Failure to manage the risks in any of these areas, and the many other ventures within a company, leads to loss and, in extreme cases, can result in their failure. It is clear that, without the effective management of risk, companies can literally go bust in a very short space of time, as we saw when the dotcom boom turned rapidly to bust and when Nick Leeson took down Barings Bank (now immortalized in the film *Rogue Trader*).

Interest in risk management has certainly grown over the last few years and its increasing significance has ensured that it has moved up the corporate agenda. Although there are a number of reasons for this, the principal reason is the demand for more effective corporate governance from a wide range of stakeholders, including:

● institutional shareholders

● non-governmental organizations

● insurance funds

● private shareholders

● employees, especially in relation to workers' councils

- trade unions

- the press

- single-focus pressure groups

- professional bodies

- regulatory bodies

- governments.

These groups' vociferousness has increased for a variety of reasons and not least because of the excesses of boardroom behaviour, and especially concerning pay (which has increased dramatically without the commensurate improvements in shareholder value or performance). Other reasons include the apparent disregard for the environment by major business, the inability of corporations to make wise investment decisions – often associated with poorly executed mergers and acquisi-

Smart quotes

The term 'risk management' is loaded with connotations of caution and timidity, carrying unpleasant reminders of dreary sessions with insurance agents and infuriating lectures from parents on the dangers of having a good time. People who think about risk management at all are likely to think of it as a grim necessity, at best. From another perspective, however, risk management is absolutely riveting, for it is a way to gain more power over events that can change your life. Risk management can help you to seize opportunity, not just to avoid danger. Since good risk management can mean the difference between wealth and poverty, success and failure, life and death, it is worth some of your attention.

Dan Borge

tions – and the general disregard of the employee. As a result, boards of directors have come under intense scrutiny to ensure that they and the businesses they run are behaving responsibly.

But, as we all know, pressure for improved self-regulation is not the only thing that boards of directors have to contend with. Risk management is also driven by the survival instinct. Every CEO wants to emulate Jack Welch and achieve hero status with their employees and the markets. CEOs like the power that the position provides and will do their utmost to lead their company to success. This means navigating their company through the turbulent waters of the economy, the markets in which they operate, change and a multitude of other factors. But, there is a flip side to this: just as the survival instinct can lead to great innovations and the smart taking of risk, it can as easily lead to the taking of unnecessary risks and the covering up of mistakes. Thus, we need to watch out for the warning signs of corporate failure (see 'Smart people to have on your side' on p.18).

In general, the combination of more stringent regulation and the uncertainties of the local and global economies dictate that every CEO must adopt a proactive stance to risk and risk management. Being proactive requires that they establish the basis for managing risk throughout their enterprise so that every employee is able to take those risks that are necessary to earn good returns for the business and to continue to advance its capabilities. The purpose behind risk management is therefore not about eliminating risk, as this is impossible, but about becoming more adept at spotting and dealing with those future events that could upset the business equilibrium. And it should be recognized that risk management is not just about being defensive; it is also about taking risks that will facilitate innovation and allow the business to grow (more about the relationship between innovation and risk in Chapter 8).

Smart people to have on your side: Larry Elliot and Richard Schroth

Larry Elliot, president and CEO of EDA, and Richard Schroth, a consultant and adviser on emerging technology and business strategy, are the authors of *How Companies Lie*. Elliot and Schroth believe that companies such as Enron, WorldCom, Global Crossing, Waste Management and Tyco represent just the tip of the iceberg, and they have identified the following warning signs of potential failure:

1 The mechanics of mendacity – companies begin to believe in their own hype, myths and lies and make bad decisions.
2 The art of artful dodgers – companies become expert at covering up the important facts, which would otherwise highlight their problems, by using as much misinformation as they can lay their hands on.
3 Words without foundation – companies become expert liars, always hoodwinking the audience (be they institutional shareholders, auditors or private investors); but without trust and truth there can be no long-term value.
4 The fog of corporate complexity – complexity can shield a multitude of sins, as we saw with Enron.
5 Dysfunctional governance – corporate governance is not working well, standards are inconsistent and out of touch with the way businesses operate.

We should recognize that the importance of risk is a matter of perspective. Where you sit within an organization's hierarchy will determine which risks will concern you. The same is true of your functional role. For example, if you are operationally focused and work, say, within a manufacturing plant, it is unlikely that you will be required to manage strategic risks. Equally, if your role is to deliver change into an organization through projects and programmes, your primary focus will be the management of project-related risks. Thus, when it comes to establishing an effective risk management framework for the organization as a whole, it is important for this to encapsulate the complete panoply of risks that require management.

Smart voices: The South Sea Bubble[1]

Since 1688 England had been in an almost constant state of war with the French. As a result, national debt had spiralled out of control and so had taxes. In order to address this terrible state of affairs, Parliament established the Bank of England in 1694. Its purpose would be to lend money to government in return for 8 per cent interest per year. It was also allowed to print its own money in order to manage the debt. However, by 1710 the government owed £8 million. With nowhere to turn, a new approach was needed.

On 10 September 1711, the South Sea Company was formally created as a mechanism to reduce Britain's national debt and, as its backers hoped, rival the Bank of England. The company would ask the government's creditors to exchange the money they were owed for shares in the South Sea Company. In addition, and in order to service the interest on the debt, the company would be paid £500,000 a year by the government. The company would export a multitude of goods, including silk, cheese and slaves, to raise revenue.

As expected, there was enormous interest from investors who bought thousands of pounds' worth of shares, believing they would make their fortune. Before long, the company had become a financial corporation to float the national debt, even though it had made no money from slaves or wool. The new monarch, George I, was convinced to invest in the company and by 1715 it had several thousand shareholders. Then, in 1719, the company was allowed to convert additional government debt into shares and the company's capital grew to be in excess of £12 million. Still the company had made no profit from any of its activities.

By 1720 government debt had risen to £31 million and the South Sea Company was keen to take this on, because it believed the greater the debt, the greater the profit from selling shares in the national debt. The profits were potentially enormous so long as the share price continued to rise. However, in order to take on such debt there had to be agreement from Parliament. After a seemingly tortuous debate, the South Sea Bill was passed and the share price rose to 400. In order to maintain and increase the share price the company instigated a number of schemes, including bribes and lending money to potential investors to purchase shares. In other words, investors' money was being recycled to bolster the stock.

The company's success had also spurred a number of similar schemes (in the same way that the early dotcoms did) – everyone wanted a piece of the action. But everyone was unaware of the risks they were running. By early June 1720 shares in the South Sea Company stood at 830, as the company spent investors' money as quickly as they received it. The bubble couldn't last and those that foresaw its demise exited, along with their handsome profits. The company was not deterred and continued to offer more and more shares to the unsuspecting public. The share price rose to above 1100, valuing the company at more than £300 million – ten times the debt it was holding. And still no ships went anywhere near the South Seas. Unfortunately, its shareholders owed it almost £60 million, double the original debt and possibly more than the wealth of the entire nation.

Public confidence was shaken when the government took action against the South Sea Company's rivals. Stocks plummeted, and investors were saddled with large debts, which could only be repaid by selling their shares in the South Sea Company. The selling depressed the share price. Attempts at bolstering the share price by launching additional share offers were initially successful as the power of the bubble was holding out. Then, in a fit of pique, the company announced a dividend of 30 per cent, which implied annual profits of £15 million, which was patently absurd.

Finally, the truth was out: investors realized that the company had no trading prospects, that the annual profits of £15 million were nonsensical and the South Sea Company was not a proper company at all. The rout had begun. The share price dropped and by early September 1720 was down to 180. Nearly every notable family in England had been caught out and many were ruined by their losses. Some even took their own life. The impact on the economy was significant and lasted for many years. It took the stock market almost 100 years to recover.

A short history of risk[2]

> **Smart quotes**
>
> Nothing in life is certain. In everything we do, we gauge the chances of successful outcomes, from business to medicine to the weather. But for most of human history, probability, the formal study of the laws of chance, was used for only one thing. Gambling.
>
> Larry Gonick

There should be no doubt that without an understanding of risk we would not be living in the complex world we now inhabit. We would not have been able to advance science to the extent that we have, develop the concept of life assurance against which we can provide financial security for those who are left behind after our deaths, or travel into space. Despite the complaints that life is getting too complex to cope with, it is fair to say that we are more equipped to cope with it than our forebears were because of our tacit understanding of the world around us and of risk management.

This is a far cry from the world of our ancestors, who had little grasp of the world around them and no real concept of how to navigate through their short and usually difficult and brutal lives. And we do not need to go that far back to reach a time when people placed their lives in the hands of the gods and the soothsayers who purported to do their bidding. Few could comprehend what the future would hold for them on a daily basis, let alone a year or decade ahead. They would pray for the return of the growing season, for the sun to reappear the next day after setting in the evening, and place magical powers in animals, celestial events, sacrifices and those among them that appeared more knowledgeable. Our ancestors did not understand the concept of risk, and neither did they understand the concept of the future – both go hand-in-hand.

Irrespective of how well we manage risk, the very fact that it is part of our common language is due to the culmination of thousands of years of evolution, insight and research covering numbering systems, probability, sampling, and the normal distribution.

The evolution of risk began with the development of numbering systems. After all, without numbers there could be no management of risk because it would be impossible to assess the probability of an event. Counting is, of course, easy with fingers, and nearly all ancient populations were able to count to ten very easily, but not much further – although you could argue that it would be possible to reach twenty by using all your fingers and toes. There is in fact one tribe in New Guinea that uses combinations of hands and feet to define numbers.

According to historians, our ability to count probably started some 4000 years ago and primarily for religious reasons. One of the best examples is Stonehenge in the UK, which was constructed around 1800 BC to allow pagan priests to calculate the frequency of natural events, in this case the summer and winter solstices. But counting, although useful, was not helpful because there was no convenient system that would allow numbers to be displayed. The first major advance was the introduction of simple symbols that could represent numbers, such as how many people lived in the village, head of cattle and so on, and such systems were typified by lines in sand or notches on wood. Unfortunately, these became cumbersome even at relatively small values.

The next leap forward was the invention of the place-value notational system of multiples of ten. This system of numbering used the additive law in which the sequence of symbols could be added together, as with Roman numerals (XXII would become 10 + 10 + 1 + 1 = 22). But this too was problematic as it was difficult to manipulate large numbers, and symbols did not lend themselves to the discovery of probability and calculus. Of course, the Romans were not alone in this. The Egyptians, for example, used a combination of vertical lines for numbers up to and including nine and symbols thereafter. For instance, a lotus flower was used to represent 1000 and a pointing finger for 10,000. Other ancient civilizations, including the Babylonians, Mayans and Grecians, had their equivalents.

It wasn't until the Hindus developed their numbering system around AD 500, on which ours is based today, that things really advanced. The central component to its success was the use of zero. This revolutionized our ability to manipulate numbers in two ways. First, it was possible to use only ten digits (from zero to nine) to create every conceivable number and, second, it made the numbering system visible and clear to everyone. This allowed the field of mathematics to advance considerably, particularly during the Renaissance.

One of the main interests of many thinkers and early mathematicians at this time was the game of chance. For example, the Franciscan monk Luca Paccioli was interested in determining how to settle an incomplete game of Balla. The game was stopped at five games to three (the winner would have been declared on winning six games). This conundrum proved to be very significant because it marked the beginnings of the detailed and systematic analysis of probability, which as we know lies at the heart of risk. Many people followed Paccioli, including Cardano, Galileo, Pascal and Fermat, all of who helped to advance the underlying concepts of probability and, of course, risk.

John Graunt, who in 1662 published a book that addressed births and deaths in London between 1604 and 1661, did much to advance the concept of statistics and is considered by some to be the father of this field of mathematics. He recognized that the information he had about London's population was only a fraction of the total; in other words, he was working with a sample and drawing wider conclusions from it, especially in terms of London's total population. He also began to use the data he had collected to predict the ages at which people would die. Such sampling was at the heart of the emergent insurance industry that started in the coffee houses of London during the second half of the seventeenth century, when trade between England and the colonies grew significantly.

Edward Lloyd opened his business in 1687 and this soon became extremely popular, with it open almost 24 hours a day to cope with demand. Lloyd launched his now famous list in 1696. This was populated with news and information about shipping routes, weather and other intelligence through a network of correspondents in the major ports. The people who would frequent Lloyd's and the other coffee houses were risk takers, those willing to underwrite the ships and their cargos. It wasn't long before the insurance industry had expanded beyond shipping.

The first serious analysis of risk was made by the Swiss mathematician Daniel Bernoulli in 1738. Bernoulli drew the distinction between games and real life by observing how people view probability and hence risk. Unlike in games, where people are less concerned about outcomes, in every day life people will try to maximize the expected utility of the outcome (in other words, they will weight it) and will be more concerned about the outcome of any risk they take. He also stated that people will assign different values to risk depending on their own psychological make-up. Therefore, those who are more willing to take risks will tend to follow a high-risk high-return policy and those who want to avoid negative outcomes will avoid risk as much as they can. This helps to explain why some people are more risk averse than others.

Other members of the Bernoulli family continued to take an interest in risk and probability, but it was De Moivre, a Frenchman who fled to London following the renewed persecution of protestants by King Louis XIV, who made the next leap forward with the creation of what we now call the normal distribution. The bell curve, as it is often known, enabled him to calculate a statistical measure of dispersion around the mean and became one of the principal ways of evaluating the probability that a given number of observations would fall within a particular population of data. And as we all know, the normal distribution forms the core of most systems of risk management. But as we will see, risk management is not just about the normal distribution, as those who seek to exploit and profit from risks will seek out events that fall outside the normal patterns of life.

Since the fundamentals of risk were discovered, there has been a significant push to make their application more sophisticated in order to deal with the increased complexities of life. In the main, these have focused on financial instruments, such as derivatives and hedging, rather than on the mainstream application of risk within organizations. Risk management has now become a profession in its own right. In every organization you now see a plethora of people whose role is almost exclusively focused on the management of risk, including:

- internal auditors

- chief risk officers

- compliance officers

- credit risk officers

- environmental risk officers

- health and safety officers.

Others too are focused on risk, but not necessarily on a full-time basis. Such people include:

- chief financial officers

- chief operating officers

- project managers

- programme managers

- corporate treasurers

- operational managers.

Furthermore, there are consultancies and third-party suppliers that provide expert risk management advice and support, which ranges from environmental risk management through to project and programme risks. And, of course, there are the tools, techniques and software systems that allow organizations to manage their risks as effectively as possible.

Risk management is now big business and we continue to advance its application. Our love affair with risk and risk management has spanned hundreds of years and, since the destruction of the Twin Towers and the demise of Enron, it has taken on an even greater significance (see Table 1.1 for a summary of the key events that have framed our understanding of risk and risk management).

History is undoubtedly important, but at the heart of risk management lies probability, and the failure to grasp this essential concept is the cause of many misconceptions and errors of judgement. It is this to which we will now briefly turn.

Table 1.1   Key events

AD	Event
500	Hindus develop the numbering system we use today
1200	Hindu–Arabic numbering system reaches the West
1494	Franciscan monk Luca Paccioli publishes *Summa de arithmetic, geometria et proportionalita* (very great abstraction and subtlety of mathematics), which introduces the concept of double-entry bookkeeping
1545	Girolamo Cardano publishes *Ars Magna* (Great Art), the first work to concentrate on algebra
1565	Girolamo Cardano writes, but fails to publish, *Liber de Ludo Aleae* (Book on Games and Chance), which develops the statistical principles of probability
1657	Huygens publishes a book on probability
1662	Port-Royal monastery publishes *Logic*, which discusses philosophy and probability. The last four chapters of the book are dedicated to probability and include a description of a game in which ten players risk one coin in the hope of winning the coins of the others
c.1670	John Graunt publishes a distribution of life expectancy from ages 6 to 76 that provides the inspiration for the UK's Central Statistical Office
1675	Emergence of coffee houses in the City of London which were used to swap news and information about sailing times, weather conditions and such like for merchant shipping
1693	Edmund Halley publishes *Transactions,* in which he calculates annuity rates based on life expectancy. This will form the basis for the future life insurance industry
1696	Edward Lloyd launches the Lloyd's list that contained details on the arrivals and departures of ships, and conditions abroad and at sea. The list was later expanded to include daily information on stock prices, foreign markets and high-water times at London Bridge
1733	Abraham De Moivre publishes *Doctrine of Chances*, which introduces the normal distribution (bell curve) that allowed him to calculate the dispersion about the mean of a set of observations (the standard deviation). This provided the basis of the assessment of an event's probability
1738	Daniel Bernouilli publishes a paper that discusses the new theory on the measurement of risk

AD	Event
1801	Carl Friedrich Guass publishes *Disquistiones Arithmeticae*, which discusses the theory of numbers
1820–1853	Lambert Quetelet publishes three books on probability
1933	Glass-Steagall Act separates commercial banking from investment banking activities
1936	John Maynard Keynes publishes the *General theory of employment interest and money*
1952	Portfolio selection revolutionizes the process of investment management by elevating risk to equal importance with expected return
1960	James Tobin and Bill Sharpe design the Capital Asset Pricing Model (CAPM)
1972	The Mercantile Exchange in Chicago creates the International Money Market that specializes in foreign currency futures and options on futures on major currencies
1982	Options on fixed income securities introduced
1990	Equity index swaps introduced
1992	COSO and Cadbury control standards introduced; differential swaps introduced
1996	CoBiT control standard introduced
2002	New legislation (the Sarbanes-Oxley Act) is introduced to avoid the accounting irregularities associated with Enron, WorldCom and others. Under the new laws, CEOs and finance directors will have to sign off their accounts as true statements. If these prove to be wrong, they can face long jail sentences. In addition, the time to close the books and report accounts will be reduced significantly by 2005
2003	The Higgs Report in the UK recommends the separation of the chairman's and chief executive's role, the appointment of a senior non-executive director who should be available to shareholders, the widening of the pool of independent directors and the development and disclosure of policies on induction training for new directors, continuing professional development and board evaluation

Smart answers to tough questions

Q. When it comes to risk management, what are you …

- a fatalist – willing to react to events without any prior thinking or activity;
- a fanatic – believing that there are no risks to manage, as you have total faith in your abilities to achieve whatever you want to achieve;
- a pessimist – never willing to take any risks because of a strong fear of failure; or
- a pragmatist – understanding that there is balance between risk and reward and that risks have to be carefully identified and actively managed?

A. It is clear that being a pragmatist achieves the right balance between risk and reward. Blindly believing that you can change the world, or take unnecessary risks (the fanatic), is destined to failure. We saw this with the dotcom boom, when its proponents stated that the Old Economy was dead. The reverse was true. Just as bad is believing in fate – what will be, will be – as this is an equally poor way to manage risk. The fatalists will do little to assess and manage risk and they roll with the punches. And not taking any risk at all, as with the pessimist, ensures that there is no advancement or opportunity to grow. The optimum approach is to take the stance of the pragmatist, who recognizes that risk is a balance that requires an intelligent approach to its management. Unfortunately most organizations contain few pragmatists but plenty of fanatics, fatalists and pessimists. This has to change.

Probability – the heart of risk management

The purpose of this section is to provide a brief summary of the key aspects of probability, as they affect the way organizations manage risk. I cannot hope to cover the subject in any great depth, as there is not the space. However, I hope there is enough here for you to understand its importance to the management of risk and, more importantly, start to recognize some of the pitfalls and problems that occur when we do not understand what probabilistic statements actually mean and what healthchecks need to be applied to them. All too often, we accept them at face value when we shouldn't.

Understanding risk management requires us to get to grips with some basic definitions of certainty, uncertainty and probability. The *Oxford Reference Dictionary* defines each as:

- Certainty – 'an undoubted fact; an indubitable prospect … absolute conviction.'

- Probability – 'being probable; likelihood … something that is probable, the most probable event … the extent to which an event is likely to occur, measured by the ratio of favourable cases to all possible cases.'

- Uncertainty – 'being uncertain; any of various similar restrictions on the accuracy of measurement.'

> You cannot escape the responsibility of tomorrow by evading it today.
>
> Abraham Lincoln

Smart quotes

A tendency to drastically underestimate the frequency of coincidences is a prime characteristic of innumerates, who generally accord great significance to correspondences of all sorts while attributing too little significance to quite conclusive but less flashy statistical evidence.

John Allen Paulos

These definitions help, in so far as they clarify the distinction between certainty and uncertainty and where probability might fit into this spectrum. But we all tend to get a little confused about the relationship between probability and certainty. Very often we believe that a probability is somehow an indication of certainty, when it is really providing us with an indication of how likely an outcome may be, given a set of factors.

A risk, by definition, has a degree of uncertainty associated with it. If an event were certain, there would be no risk, as it would occur, no matter what we did to prevent it. Unfortunately, most of the population suffers from fuzzy thinking when it comes to risk and uncertainty. Much of this fuzziness is generated by the way in which risks and statistics are presented in the press, which perpetuates the problem. According to Sharon Friedman, Professor of the Department of Journalism and Communication at Leigh University,[3] the media make limited use of actual numbers when describing risks. Words such as safe and unsafe, or low and high, are used but without any clarification of what they actually mean in real terms. They also create simple causal links between a factor, such as toxic waste, and, say, birth defects, but without taking into account the other wide-ranging factors that can also lead to birth defects, such as genetic predisposition, smoking, alcohol abuse, drug abuse and diet. This tardiness helps to excite people's concerns about the health hazards of toxic waste, and the environment in general. If this approach were used in scientific study, the results would be laughed out of any self-respecting journal.

Similar problems arise when the media presents information pertaining to our diets and what we should and shouldn't eat. Take fat, for example, and its links to levels of cholesterol in our bloodstream. We should not eat butter and instead opt for low-fat spreads. But low-fat spreads are not necessarily good for us either and the direct correlation between fat and high levels of cholesterol in our bloodstream has not been proven conclusively. Indeed, look at the current obsession with the Atkins Diet. This seems to fly in the face of convention because it recommends the consumption of fat and protein to the exclusion of everything else. People swear by it but, like everything else, there is a flip side. In Atkins case it is kidney stones and even premature death. What this proves is that in order to weigh up any risk we need all the relevant information, not just that which is interesting or controversial.

The media's misrepresentation of risk helps to foster the general ignorance in the wider population, which includes businesses as much as the general public. Our ability to understand risk depends almost entirely on our grasp of probability. Without this we can fall into a number of traps, including those highlighted by Gerd Gigerenzer, as follows.[4]

The illusion of certainty

We are often seduced by statistics and will believe that an event described in statistical terms is more certain than it actually is. This is because we take the information at face value rather than assessing it more intelligently. In other words, we are not able to understand just how certain or uncertain something is. For example, we have been reading for some time that there is a link between the mumps, measles and rubella (MMR) triple vaccination that is given to young children and autism. Doctors and researchers continue to publish and debate the issue very publicly, using statistical evidence to back up their conflicting viewpoints. The reaction from the public has been somewhat typical, with many refusing to vaccinate their children because of this alleged link. As a result, there is now an increase in the childhood diseases the MMR vaccination was meant to prevent, especially in cities, where the transmission of disease is generally easier.

People will believe the statistical evidence without understanding what the actual risk is because they fail to place the information into the wider population of children having the inoculation. Although there might be a link (which itself is uncertain and for anyone following the debate is still inconclusive), the chances of a child contracting autism are believed to be remote. Interestingly, there has been a knock-on effect from the MMR debacle which has involved doctors removing babies and young children from their registers so that they are still able to meet government targets for inoculation. This illustrates the systemic nature of risks very neatly – an action will always have a consequence elsewhere.

The same sorts of attitudes are evident with terrorism. Again this is a remote risk, but most of us, and especially those who work in cities or are frequent flyers, believe that it is more likely than it is. I know of people who are unwilling to fly because of the events of September 11th and yet the risk associated with being killed in a terrorist-related incident is highly remote. As I stated in the introduction, we are more likely to be killed in a car crash than die in a terrorist attack. But, as we saw above, the treatment of risks by the media reinforces our sense of paranoia. I saw this first hand when presenting at a conference on risk just before the Second Gulf War. The US participants pulled out at the last minute because they believed they would be a target of terrorist attack as they flew across the Atlantic.

Contrast this with when a colleague and I were in the Sudan on September 11th. This was a country that had harboured Bin Laden and was bombed by the USA in 1998. Having witnessed the destruction of the Twin Towers on CNN 200 miles south of Khartoum, our families were clearly concerned. After all, we were in a Muslim country, which was believed to be associated with terrorist activities. Our view was very different. We weighed up the risk very carefully, taking into account the run-up to the First Gulf War, where it took months before the coalition had been built and was ready for war. It was clear that the risk to ourselves was remote. So, we stayed on and completed our assignment, which we did without any problem. Judgement is of paramount importance in managing risk. All too often it is lacking.

Ignorance of risk

This point follows from the last in so far as our failure to interpret the underlying numbers associated with statistics and probability ensures that we have difficulty in understanding how significant the risks we face actually are.

Miscommunication of risk

If we do not understand the nature of numbers and probability then it should come as no surprise that we cannot communicate them in a way that other people can understand. Gigerenzer cites an example of a doctor who, when he prescribed Prozac to his patients, would inform them of the risks associated with a loss of sexual desire. To begin with he would tell them that they had a 30 to 50 per cent chance of losing their sexual appetite. Many believed, quite wrongly, that they would lose it for up to 50 per cent of the time. Even so, no one bothered to ask what it meant to them; they assumed. He then changed tack and told his patients that out of every ten patients, between three and five would experience problems. This resolved the issue and, as a result, patients were more likely to ask questions and be clearer about the risks they faced.

Clouded thinking

This final trap is associated with our inability to draw conclusions from the risks that we face. Even though we may know what the risks are, we are unable to draw the necessary conclusions. This is particularly evident within medical testing. Patients and clinicians wrongly assume that the results of, say, a blood screen, a cervical smear or any other such test are conclusive. There are occasions where the tests come back as a false positive; in other words, they are wrong because of human or computer error. There are a number of instances where complete batches of smear tests for women have been found to be false, causing huge scares among those patients who have been given a clean bill of health as much as those who had been told they had cancer. A particularly insidious example is that of Therac-25, in which the operator of the system insisted to a patient, who had just been administered an unusually high dose of radiation, that the equipment could not have given an overdose because it was computer controlled. In other words, there was no risk of an overdose, which of course was patently wrong as it was later found that there was a subtle error in the software which was eventually linked to a number of deaths.

Smart people to have on your side: John Allen Paulos

John Allen Paulos is Professor of Mathematics and Presidential Scholar at Temple University, Philadelphia, and the author of *Innumeracy: Mathematical illiteracy and its consequences*. Paulos believes that innumeracy (the inability to deal comfortably with the fundamental notions of number and chance) plagues too many people and he asserts that failing to have a feeling for large numbers and probabilities ensures that people misunderstand the significance of the risks they face.

So, how do we avoid the traps identified by Gerd Gigerenzer? The trick is to understand some of the basic principles associated with probability.

In very simple terms, probability helps us to describe uncertainty by providing us with the language and mathematical notation with which to deal with it. We can view an event in probabilistic terms as falling between the two poles of certainty – certainty that an event will never occur and certainty that it will. Probability is usually expressed in numerical terms which range between 0 and 1, where 0 equates to a situation that is impossible and 1 to a situation that is certain. This is represented as $0 \leq p \leq 1$, where p is probability. Probabilities are also expressed in percentages, with the 0 representing zero per cent and the 1, 100 per cent.

We all tend to be familiar with the rudimentary aspects of probability. For example, we know that there is a one in two (or 50 per cent) chance of a coin turning up either heads or tails if we toss it. Similarly, we know that if we rolled a die, a six would have a one in six (16.66 per cent) chance of being rolled. But when we start to deal with more than just coins and dice we tend to lose the plot. This is partly because of the added complexity and partly because many of the risks we face in organizations are not based upon the collection of large amounts of historical data or statistical modelling. Many risks we face are un-bounded by known extremes.

Few people really appreciated the risks associated with the rise of the dotcoms. Businesses did not recognize the risks relating to a sudden loss of highly talented people and the dotcoms themselves failed to ap-preciate the risks associated with having no effective business model. They assumed that the money would flow forever, which of course it didn't. There are of course organizations, functions and people that apply the core principles of probability on a daily basis, including market research agencies, actuaries, investment bankers, medical researchers and government statisticians to name but a few. Other organizations, such as credit agencies and credit card companies, use it in the measurement and management of fraud-related risks. But for those of us who use these principles all but very occasionally, we ought to keep some of the basic tenets fresh in our minds.

For our purposes we should understand that probability could be one of the following:

Subjective probability

This depends on the application of judgement of the person making an estimate. Such statements usually have no basis in statistical model-ling, as there is no population of data on which to base the estimate. We are not dealing with a repeatable event. A lot of risk management, especially within business, is therefore subjective in nature. For ex-ample, project and programme risk depends almost exclusively on the project manager's experience and expertise. Given that most projects are unique events, the risks tend to be unique. However, we do know from information collected about projects the likelihood of their failure, which is around 66 per cent (or a two in three chance).

Conditional probability

Here the probability of an event is related to another. So, for example, if we wanted to know the probability that a smoker is also an alcoholic, we would have to first select all smokers and then ascertain whether they were also alcoholics. In other words, the outcome would be conditional on the person being a smoker. We would not be interested in just alcoholics.

Conditional probability can confuse. Gerd Gigerenzer provides this example:

If a woman has breast cancer, the probability that she will test positive on a screening mammogram is 90 per cent. Many mortals, physicians included, confuse that statement with this one: If a woman tests positive on a screening mammogram, the probability that she has breast cancer is 90 per cent. That is, the conditional probability that an event A occurs given event B is confused with the conditional probability that an event B occurs given an event A. This is not the only confusion. Others mistake the probability of A given B with the probability of A and B.

Relative probability

This, as the name suggests, is the probability of an event occurring relative to the total number of events. This is best illustrated by flipping a coin. If we flip a coin 50 times and it comes up heads 20 times then the relative probability will be 20 divided by 50, giving 0.4, or 40 per cent. Relative probabilities tend to crop up in medical and scientific experiments.

Complementary probability

If the probability of being knocked down by a bus was 0.3 (or approximately one in three) then we could state that the chances of not being knocked down would be 0.7. This is the complementary probability and is simple to calculate as it involves subtracting the probability of the given event from 1 (100 per cent certainty). We often look at risks in this way when weighing up the outcomes of a particular event. Returning to the project example, we would know that if two-thirds of projects failed, one-third should succeed.

Independent probability

We should recognize that events are not always dependent on each other. If we take the UK's Lotto game, a player has approximately a 1 in 14 million chance of winning. If, after a draw, the same balls were placed back into the container and drawn again, the two events would be independent. In other words, your chances of winning would remain the same because the second draw would not be influenced by the first.

In addition to the above, we should also get a bit more familiar with such things as populations, the normal distribution and standard deviations, if only to understand their significance in relation to risk.

Taking populations first, when we read that 67 per cent of men like football we may assume that every single man in the country has been canvassed as to their views on football. This is of course untrue, as this approach would be both expensive and time consuming. A sample of men will have been questioned, but certainly not all. If this subset of the total number of men is of a sufficient size, it can be classed as statistically significant. In other words, it is of a sufficient size and diversity as to provide a reasonable representation of the complete male population (it should sample a wide age profile, socio-economic make-up

Smart quotes

Making probability judgements has become very important in the modern world. For example, courts (and juries) are asked to make judgements about whether particular disabilities are related to occupational exposures or environmental hazards for which organizations are responsible. Since there is simply no way of saying 'this cancer was for sure caused by that exposure,' instead experts argue about the probabilities that people exposed develop cancer as opposed to the probability that someone not exposed develops cancer. Another example involves environmental impact statements for new, private or public projects or products. There can be no justifiable statement about *exactly* what the impacts will be; instead we must make some probability judgements about how likely various impacts are to occur.

Robyn Dawes

and location). It is important to know this as it will help us to draw any conclusions. If the population on which the statistics are based is too small, we could end up deriving the wrong conclusion and taking actions that will lead to problems and potential failure down the line.

Market research organizations, such as Mori, take great care to ensure their samples are statistically significant. But how many times do we read about the probability of contracting such things as heart disease or cancer from particular foods, or how certain foodstuffs can prevent disease, without checking the size of the population from which these conclusions have been drawn. An associated factor with medical statistics is the length of studies, as this too is very important. Medical studies take place over many years, often decades, in order to ensure there is confidence in the results.

As we saw earlier, it was De Moivre who first recognized the normal distribution and its important characteristics. The normal distribution is a bell-shaped curve that is perfectly symmetrical, hence its common name, the bell curve (see Fig. 1.1). When looking at any graph that shows a distribution, it is possible to estimate the mode (the value with the highest frequency) and median (the middle point) visually. It is harder to estimate the mean, however, as this depends on the range of values within the distribution. But within the normal distribution the mean coincides with the mode and median so, in this case, the mean, mode and median all have the same value.

Because the mean is at the centre of the curve, 50 per cent of the observations fall either side of it. The normal curve is characterized by the relationship between the mean and the standard deviation (the standard deviation is a measure of how spread out your data is across the sample – see 'Smart answers to tough questions', p.42). This allows us to determine the proportion of the data within a certain range – classified by the standard deviation. The distance between the mean and one standard deviation will include 68 per cent of all observations; 95 per cent of the observations will fall within two standard deviations; and 99.7 per cent will fall within three standard deviations. This is illustrated in Fig. 1.2.

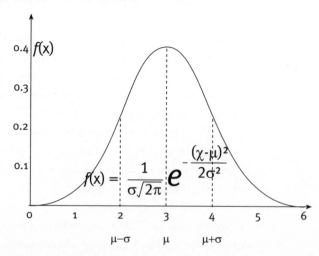

$$f(x) = \frac{1}{\sigma\sqrt{2\pi}} e^{-\frac{(x-\mu)^2}{2\sigma^2}}$$

Fig. 1.1 The normal distribution

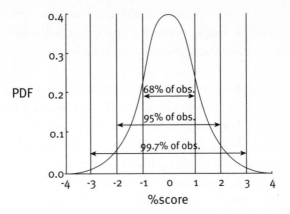

Fig. 1.2 Standard deviations

Therefore, once you know the mean and standard deviation of the bell curve you can estimate what proportion of a sample's observations will fall above or below a particular value or between two values. This is helpful to risk managers because it provides them with an indication of the likelihood of a risk occurring. Clearly, if an event falls outside three standard deviations, it will be unlikely to occur, but if it falls within one standard deviation, it has a high probability of occurring.

Thus, the normal distribution and its unique characteristics can be helpful to those risk managers who rely on historical data to assess their risks. Indeed, this lies at the heart of financial risk management and is particularly important in trading environments, such as investment banking. Naturally, the sophistication of the risk management tools used within these environments goes far beyond the rudimentary analysis provided here and there are plenty of books that deal with these tools exclusively, so I do not intend to discuss these any further. What I hope to have illustrated here is the importance of understanding probability and how a basic grasp of the normal distribution will help the risk manager make a more intelligent assessment of risk. I also hope that it has illustrated several of the pitfalls associated with some of the clouded thinking that surrounds probabilistic statements and, as a result, forearmed you with questions you might want to ask before accepting information at face value.

Risk management has evolved to become one of the core disciplines of every organization. It touches on a lot of what we do in our daily lives and yet we seem to be oblivious to its significance. It is clear to me that people in general – and those with responsible positions within organizations – do not appreciate the underlying concepts of risk management and, as a result, tend to make errors of judgement. Risk management is, as we know, an essential discipline within any company, irrespective of its size. If this is the case, organizations have

Smart answers to tough questions

Q. How do you calculate the standard deviation and what can it tell us?

A. The standard deviation is calculated in the following way:

1   Compute the mean for the data set.
2   Compute the deviation by subtracting the mean from each value.
3   Square each individual deviation.
4   Add up the squared deviations.
5   Divide by one less than the sample size.
6   Take the square root.
7   This is the standard deviation.

The standard deviation shows how spread out the bell curve is. So, if the standard deviation is one, the curve will be tall and thin, which implies the data is very concentrated and has little variation. If the standard deviation is two, the curve will be flatter and more spread out. This implies that there is greater variation in the data. Finally, if the standard deviation is three, the curve will be flatter still and have the greatest variation in the data.

to become smarter at understanding and managing risks, which is the purpose of this book. But before we can turn to the smart thinking that is required to manage risks more effectively, we must first spend some time understanding the wide-ranging nature of risk within the typical corporation. This is the subject of the next chapter.

Notes

1   For a full account of the South Sea Bubble, see Balen, M. (2002) *A Very English Deceit: The Secret History of the South Sea Bubble and the First Great Financial Scandal*, London: Fourth Estate.

2   This section is sourced from a collection of articles and books that cover the history of numbers and risk. The most notable of these are: *A Short History of Numbers*, which can be found at www.giance.com; *A Short History of Ancient Numerals*, which can be found at www.math.byu.edu; and Bernstein, P. (1996) *Against the Gods: The Remarkable Story of Risk*, New York: John Wiley & Sons.

3   Friedman, S. (2002) *The media, risk assessment and numbers: They don't add up*, www.piercelaw.edu/risk/vol5/summer/friedman.htm.

4   Gigerenzer, G. (2002) *Reckoning With Risk: Learning to Live With Uncertainty*, London: Allen Lane, The Penguin Press, pp. 24–5.

2 Categories of Risk

Over time, the nature of risk has mutated. No longer restricted to financial risk, it extends into any venture where there is a degree of uncertainty and possibility of loss. Although it is perfectly feasible to dream up a large number of risk categories, I believe that the following cover the majority of those we face in the course of our working and non-working lives:

1 financial

2 strategic

3 programme and project

4 operational

5 environmental

6 technological

7 brand

8 reputational

9 talent

10 personal.

As a classification it helps those who are required to manage risk, because without such stratification there is a real danger that risk can become non-specific. This makes it difficult to manage and results in people discussing risk in vague and undefined terms. Articulation is an essential stage in the risk management process and one that is frequently overlooked (more on this in Chapter 4). I have also included personal risk within this categorization because I believe we are generally poor at understanding the risks we face as individuals. Indeed, there is an increasing propensity to live for the moment rather than considering the longer-term consequences of our actions. This is often borne out in our careers, finances and, increasingly, our retirement planning.

Although this categorization helps in the management of discrete risks, in order to be successful, organizations need to manage risk in an integrated fashion. In practice this means understanding how the various categories of risk interact. This is something I will discuss in Chapter 4. The purpose of this chapter is to ensure the reader understands enough about the types of risk they face so that they can articulate them more readily and undertake further research and reading as necessary. The remainder of this chapter explores each of the ten categories in some, but not immense, detail.

Smart things to say about risk management

If you can't articulate risk, you can't manage it.

Financial risk

As we saw in Chapter 1, risk management as a business discipline evolved from the need to model the financial risks of the emerging insurance industry. This soon spread into the fledgling stock markets of the seventeenth century and latterly into the wider business environment. As to be expected, financial risk is one of the most complex areas of risk management, continuously evolving as the nature of financial markets have changed. Modelling and managing financial risks involves the application of sophisticated analysis tools based on complex mathematical models.

Most organizations tend to be reasonably adept at managing their financial risks although, as we have seen with Enron, Tyco and other high-profile accounting scandals, in some cases this has meant cooking the books rather than being open and honest. But these are difficult times. Stock markets around the world have been suffering. Since the imploding of the technology bubble in 2000, stock markets have dropped year after year. With three years of falls, the current bear market is the worst since the Great Depression between 1929 and 1931. During the Depression the Dow–Jones fell by almost 90 per cent. Although not quite as bad, the Dow–Jones had, at its lowest point in early 2003, fallen almost 50 per cent from its peak.

Similar reductions have been experienced by all the major indices across the world and, although every analyst believes that a fourth year of stock market contraction is unprecedented, there are those who believe that the overhang of debt, limited investment and wrong-footed government intervention will ensure that stock market growth will be stunted for the foreseeable future. And we should also recognize that previous years' falls are unrelated statistically. In other words, each year is independent of the last and because the last three years have fallen, a rise in the fourth cannot be guaranteed. After all, every year has a 38 per cent chance of falling irrespective of what occurred in the previous year. As I write this book, the markets are finally re-covering, mainly because of the stability that has returned following the ending of the Second Gulf War. We will have to wait and see if the bears or bulls reign supreme over the coming years.

A falling market presents major issues for every quoted company because:

- it makes it harder for them to raise debt;

- it can result in them becoming a target for takeover; and

- it results in a reduction in their credit rating, thereby making their debt more costly to service.

More worryingly, many companies are facing significant difficulties in covering their pension liabilities, which is the result of the combination of falling stock markets and ageing populations. According to the UK's CBI, falling share prices have left businesses with a £100 billion pension fund deficit. In response, a large number have shut down their final salary schemes (which pays a pension based on a combination of the worker's number of years of pensionable service and their final salary) in favour of money purchase schemes (which places the risks on to the employees, whose pensions depend on the vagaries of the stock markets and therefore provides no guarantee of future income).

UK life assurance organizations and their customers also face difficult times because of the fall in stock values. The assurance companies' with-profits funds depend on the performance of equities which, under the current state of affairs, has led to a reduction in the bonuses paid to their clients. In extreme cases, such as the near bankruptcy of Equitable Life, pensioners have been left with next to nothing. For some it has meant delaying retirement, while for others it has resulted in, at best, only semi-retirement or, at worst, a near breadline existence. Assurance companies also have to maintain a minimum margin of 4 per cent between their reserves and liabilities, which is proving to be very difficult under the current conditions – many are technically insolvent. This in turn makes it difficult to raise new debt and service existing loans. It should therefore come as no surprise that Standard & Poor have downgraded the credit ratings of Prudential, Standard Life and a number of other major life assurance companies.

Smart quotes

What must we do to destroy the integrity of our capital markets? Nothing! The destruction is well under way. The underside of the stock market became more visible over the past five years during the frenzy of the technology and Internet bubbles. The markets, due to the lies of corporate leaders and those who surround them, are the casinos and dog tracks of this new century. The odds in Las Vegas and the odds of making money by investing in companies have two major differences. In Las Vegas, one can compute the odds of winning or losing. These days, the way publicly traded companies are behaving, you cannot. The dealers in Las Vegas do not insert or remove a couple of aces during the game, but on Wall Street and among many of the publicly traded companies, they do. At least in Las Vegas you get a good meal and free drink.

Larry Elliot and Richard Schroth

Financial risk management typically covers the following subcategories:[1]

- *Market risk*. This refers to the risk that changes in the price of stocks and/or interest rates leads to a reduction in the value of an investment portfolio or security. There are four types of market risk:

  1 Foreign exchange risk. The major sources of foreign exchange risk come from movements of currency prices and fluctuations in international interest rates. This represents one of the most significant risks for multinational organizations because it can generate huge operating losses.

2 Interest rate risk. This is the risk that the value of a fixed income security will fall because of a change in market interest rates.

3 Commodity risk. Unlike interest rate risk and foreign exchange risk, commodity risks can arise from variations in supply and demand of particular commodities, such as coffee, which can increase volatility. Commodity markets can stage dramatic changes in prices, both up and down, which also distinguishes commodity risk from other types of financial risk.

4 Equity risk. This has two components to it: the general market risk, which refers to the sensitivity of a financial instrument to the general movements in stock market indices; and specific risks, which relate to the organization itself, its sector, management capability and so on.

● *Liquidity risk*. There are two sides to this. The first is the ability of a financial institution to raise the cash it requires to meet, among other things, the collateral requirements of its counterparts and its debt. The second is the risk that an institution cannot execute a transaction at the prevailing market price because there is temporarily no appetite for the deal. If it proves to be impossible to cancel the deal then the institution can lose substantial amounts of money. It was no surprise that central banks pumped the markets with liquidity during the cutover to 2000, when the risks associated with the loss of computers due to the Millennium Bug were looming large.

● *Credit risk*. This is the risk that a counterpart defaults and the bank loses all of its market position or that part which is irrecoverable. Credit risk management is complex and institutions rely on rating agencies, such as Standard & Poor and Moody's, to provide the basic level of risk they are exposed to and hence the amount of interest they will charge. Agencies such as Moody's will analyse the company seeking credit before issuing them with a rating. Such analysis includes an assessment of the company structure, its operational and financial position, the quality of management, and any trends (market and industry) that may affect it and the wider macroeconomic environment within which the company operates.

When business transactions occur across international borders they involve additional risks beyond those that are managed in a domestic setting. This is known as country risk and it arises because of the different business, economic and political environments that exist around the world. Although some form of country risk has always been present between trading partners, globalization has emphasized the imbalances. This means that, for those organizations that are transnational, the management of country risk is an increasingly important capability. There are six main categories to country risk:[2]

- *Economic risk*. This is the risk that the expected return on an investment held/made within a country is affected by changes in a country's economic structure or growth. Such risks arise from significant changes in fiscal and monetary policy, local recessions, and resource availability.

- *Transfer risk*. This arises from restrictions in capital movements imposed by foreign governments. Such restrictions can occur during times of difficult economic or trading conditions, such as during the Asian Crisis in the late 1990s, when some Asian governments imposed fixed exchange rates to minimize the impact of falling currency values.

- *Exchange risk*. This is the risk that there is a sudden change in the value of a country's currency. Such changes are usually associated with economic turmoil, war or speculative attacks by investors (as we saw when the UK joined and subsequently left the European Exchange Rate Mechanism in 1992). Risk can also arise when a country moves from a fixed to a floating exchange rate.

- *Location or neighbourhood risk.* This, in essence, is where the problems of one country spill over to the next. This can happen in times of war (such as during the First Gulf War and more recently in the Balkans) and regional economic difficulty (as we saw in Latin America in the 1980s and Asia in the 1990s).

- *Sovereign risk.* This is the risk associated with the failure of a government to meet its loan obligations, as with Russia's default in 1998.

- *Political risk.* This relates to the general political stability of the country that can change in times of regional wars, military coups and civil war (for example, Zimbabwe).

How country risk is managed depends very much on the nature of the relationship the organization has with the countries with which it trades. For example, if it has located a manufacturing plant in another country, the risk will be long term and will require the organization to assess all aspects of the country's risk before the investment is made and for a long time after. In particular, political risks have to be carefully monitored in those parts of the world that have a history of instability. Country risk also varies with the type and nature of loans. Long-term loans to governments usually have low economic risk, but high exchange, sovereign and political risks, while a short-term loan to a private entity is typically low risk – apart from transfer risk.

The increasing sophistication and complexities of financial instruments is leading to higher risks. In particular, the rapidly expanding derivatives market is causing concern. Warren Buffett, the world's second-richest man, believes that derivatives pose a threat to both the companies that deal with them and the economy. Buffett believes that derivatives are financial weapons of mass destruction and pose a mega catastrophic risk (see 'Smart voices: Long-Term Capital Management', p.54). Derivative contracts involve a wide range of securities that typically involve a future payout that is directly linked to stock prices,

Smart people to have on your side: Dunn and Bradstreet

- Specialists in financial and credit management.
- Experts in financial risk.
- Allows business to assess their country risks using the country risk indicator, which has seven levels of risk:
  1 lowest risk
  2 low risk
  3 slight risk
  4 moderate risk
  5 high risk
  6 very high risk
  7 highest risk.

currency values or interest rates. The market for this type of financial product has increased dramatically as the volatility within the financial markets has increased.

Many organizations use derivatives to hedge against market risk and profit from movements in the securities markets and interest rates. The problem is that they can be difficult to exit from and the assumptions on which they are based can be wide of the mark. As we witnessed with Long-Term Capital Management, hedge funds can become systemically unstable when large amounts of market risk are placed in the hands of a small number of derivative dealers. For example, the Lancer Offshore Fund Group, which has lost a total of $800 million, has become the first hedge fund in history to file for Chapter 11 protection (which protects US firms from their creditors while they resolve their problems and restructure). This has impacted 108 investors, including Britney Spears and the former Sotheby's chairman.[3] More recently, a report by the Centre for Corporate Governance Research at Birmingham Business School in the UK suggested that institutional investors are turning a blind eye to companies' exposure to potentially risky financial instruments, particularly derivatives.[4]

Smart voices: Long-Term Capital Management[5]

Long-Term Capital Management was a private investment partnership headquartered in Greenwich, not far from Wall Street. The business was started in 1993 by John Meriwether, a former Solomon Brothers trader, and supported by a group of PhD-certified arbitrageurs, many of whom had been professors and two of whom had been Nobel Prize winners. For four years straight they were able to produce returns of 40 per cent per year, thus creating an illusion that they could do no wrong and that their investment strategy was pretty much risk free. Over these four years they had amassed over $100 billion in assets, nearly all of it borrowed from the major banks that comprised the global finance community. Long-Term Capital Management had also entered into thousands of derivative contracts that exposed it and the global banking community to more than $1 trillion. As long as Long-Term Capital Management did not default, there would be no problems.

Unfortunately this was not to be the case, as a number of events around the world were set to destabilize the fund and ultimately lead to its failure. The collapse of the Brazilian, Russian and Indonesian markets during the first half of 1998 resulted in a surge in market volatility, which is something that Long-Term Capital Management had not bargained for. Although it had started the year with $4.7 billion of capital, by August it had dropped to $2.9 billion, losing a third since April of the same year. Attempts to raise capital with the likes of Warren Buffett were only partially successful, as at this time the markets were still falling, there was talk of recession, everyone was running away from risk and the majority of investors wanted out of their risky investments, of which Long-Term Capital Management was one. Three-quarters of all hedge funds had lost money in August and Long-Term Capital Management lost $1.9 billion. The bad news kept coming and by 10 September the fund was below the $2 billion mark. Long-Term Capital Management now had to raise $2 billion if it was to survive.

But by now the major banks – UBS, J.P. Morgan, Merrill Lynch and others – realized that their exposures would cost them dear – between $500 million and $700 million a piece. Later that month Long-Term Capital Management's equity was down to $773 million and the only way to prevent the global finance system from collapsing was to bail out the fund. A meeting between Long-Term Capital Management and the banks was brokered by the Federal Reserve, which would not allow the fund to fail because, in its words, it was too big. The meeting was a who's who of Wall Street and was a long tortuous affair, but by the end of it 14 banks had raised $3.65 billion. In exchange they would receive 90 per cent of the equity of the fund. In less than a year the fund had dropped 91 per cent of its value.

Although recapitalized, the fund still lost more money. Within two weeks of the deal, the consortium had lost $750 million. Bank after bank wrote off their losses and suffered at the hands of the markets. The failure of Long-Term Capital Management was a lesson in risk management and greed – so often related when it comes to financial risk. The team are now back together again … will history repeat itself? They claim it won't.

Strategic risk

Strategic risk is concerned with the wider aspects of a business' activities and often encapsulates those things that are more difficult to manage and which do not fall into the other categories of risk identified above. Typically, strategic risk addresses the impacts of such things as:

● poor marketing strategy

● poor acquisitions strategy

● changes in consumer behaviour

● political and regulatory changes

● poor product launches.

The majority of strategic risk is therefore focused on ensuring that the shareholder value of an enterprise continues to grow rather than stagnate or collapse. Strategic risk management can also be viewed as the management of risks on behalf of the shareholders of a company and is, as a consequence, the responsibility of the board. According to Mercer Management Consultancy, strategic risk is concerned with one overriding question: Can the firm's business design deliver sustained, above-average growth in shareholder value? Given that the environment in which a business exists is rarely stable, strategic risk is important to both established and new companies. As we saw during the height of the dotcom boom and bust, many start-ups failed to consider their strategic positioning well enough to ensure their long-term, let alone short-term, survival.

Investors react to strategic risk both rapidly and decisively, especially since the demise of Enron, when the worst excesses of corporate greed came to light. Between May 1998 and May 2003, 10 per cent of Fortune 1000 companies lost one-quarter of their shareholder value within a one-month period after announcing reduced quarterly earnings and reductions in future earnings. The majority of these were caused by the following strategic risk factors:[6]

- drop in customer demand;

- misalignment between go-to-market channels and customer priorities; and

- increased competitive pressure.

Interestingly, others were the result of operational risks and financial risk, which illustrates quite neatly the systemic nature of risk within all modern corporations.

Killer questions

Who is looking after the future of your company and, more importantly, can you trust them?

Strategic risk also includes the more commercial risks associated with the loss of key customers, failures of suppliers and the inability of management to lead the business. The nature of the strategic risks faced by any organization will vary according to the types of markets in which it operates. For example, where the markets are heavily regulated, strategic risks will come from government intervention. This includes the finance industry and the biotech and pharmaceutical sectors as well as those sectors that have been traditionally nationalized, such as telecommunications and energy. Where businesses operate in competitive markets, the risks are likely to come from new entrants and innovations from existing players. Managing strategic risk requires that those charged with directing the business have a good understanding of the competitive landscape and, through this, they ensure that its organizational design is appropriate and aligned to address the needs of its markets and customers. One way in which organizations address this is through strategic planning.

Smart things to say about risk management

Strategic management is risk management.

The majority of business leaders recognize the value of setting strategy. Not only does it allow them to establish a clear future to which everyone in their organization can tune into, but it also ensures that investments that will change the organization are congruent with the future described in their strategy. In other words, an effective business strategy can help to mitigate some of the risks that they might face. To be effective, an organization's strategy needs to take into account a wide range of factors including:

- existing operational performance;

- the nature of the general business environment, including the national and global economies;

- competitors, which might be local, national or global;

- specific market factors that impact business viability and how these are changing;

- the technologies needed to both run an efficient operation and to develop and support new products and services; and

- the people it needs to maintain or grow market share.

Smart voices: MmO$_2$

In May 2003 MmO$_2$, the mobile phone company spun out of BT, posted the second-largest loss in corporate history at £10.2 billion, as it wrote off most of the value of its third-generation licences. Effectively, MmO$_2$ is saying that the third-generation telephony is worth less than 50 per cent of what BT paid for it.

Despite the advantages of setting and then delivering against a strategic plan, companies are still exposed to major strategic risks. A strategy cannot guarantee protection and, indeed, following a strategy can actually lead to problems. This is particularly the case in mergers and acquisitions, which so often fail (see 'Smart people to have on your side', p.59). All too often the deal sounds fantastic, and a great way to enhance market share, or to expand the scale and reach of the business. Unfortunately, the majority of mergers and acquisitions fail because of poor integration and egotistical battles in the boardroom as the prospective CEOs fight it out for the top job. (I for one have witnessed first

Smart things to say about risk management

Do you really want to acquire or merge with another company when most acquisitions and mergers fail?

Smart people to have on your side: Timothy Galpin and Mark Herndon

Galpin and Herndon are merger and acquisition specialists from Watson Wyatt Worldwide and authors of *The Complete Guide to Mergers and Acquisitions*. They assert that the majority of mergers and acquisitions fail to secure many of the strategic objectives set out at the start of the deal and outline a five-stage model that reduces the risk of failure:

1   *Formulate*, which sets the business strategy, the growth strategy, defines the acquisition criteria and begins the strategy implementation

2   *Locate*, which identifies the target markets and companies, selects the target, issues the letter of intent and develops the merger and acquisition plan

3   *Investigate*, which involves the execution of the due diligence, sets the preliminary integration plans and decides on the negotiation parameters

4   *Negotiate*, which establishes the deal terms, secures the talent and integration teams and closes the deal

5   *Integrate*, which finalizes and executes the integration plan.

hand the incompetence of senior executives and those that do their bidding – wreaking destruction rather than adding value. In fact mergers and acquisitions are two of the best ways to destroy value and waste talent.) Then of course there is the long integration tail as the cultural mismatches between the two organizations takes time to dissipate. Sometimes this never happens. During this time petty rivalries distract the organization from achieving the benefits that everyone (well, at board level at least) was hoping to achieve.

Programme and project risk

The importance of project management has grown considerably over the last 30 years. Originating in the aerospace industry during the

Smart voices: Körber[7]

Körber, a leading manufacturer, needed to diversify but was well aware of the problems associated with mergers and acquisitions, having witnessed the implosion of Marconi following a badly timed move into telecommunications equipment manufacturing. Körber wanted to avoid damaging its business. As the world's largest producer of cigarette manufacturing equipment it recognized that the future was by no means certain, especially as the awareness of the effects of smoking become more widely known.

In order to mitigate the risks it adopted an extremely rigorous process to choosing its acquisition target, which took two and a half years. During this time it explored over 300 opportunities before deciding on the acquisition that would provide the benefits it was looking for. Körber started by looking at seven industrial sectors covering information systems, chemicals, health, agriculture and food, energy and transport. After two years of searching and analysis it became clear that healthcare was the most obvious candidate. It then carried out some further analysis, screening 344 healthcare segments, all of which were focused on capital equipment. The team also visited over 30 healthcare experts to seek their opinion as to which segment Körber should opt for. Towards the end of the process (late 2001) Körber had decided to choose high technology packaging for high-value pharmaceuticals and subsequently bought a Swiss and German company.

The only way to avoid risk in the future is to change the organization in the present.

1950s when constructing large passenger planes was a major departure from traditional aircraft manufacture, project management has become an important discipline within most businesses. It is now believed that project-based work accounts for up to 30 per cent of a typical organization's activity. Projects and, increasingly, programmes are significant undertakings both in terms of expense and time. And given that they only have one chance of succeeding it should be obvious that they bring with them a high degree of risk. Increasingly projects are taking on a strategic importance within organizations, as they recognize that without them it is impossible to make the rapid changes required to survive and grow in a competitive market. Project risks will vary with the nature and objectives of the initiative but typically fall into the following categories:

- Technology. This covers those risks that relate to the technical components of the project and can include those associated with information technology, engineering, scientific experimentation and new products.

- People and behavioural. This covers those risks that relate to the changes that people have to make both in terms of their daily activities and, more importantly, in terms of their behaviours. It is a well-known fact that people resist change and that most projects and programmes fail because not enough attention is paid to the human dimension.

- Process. This encompasses those risks associated with the introduction of new processes or changes to existing ones. Processes that are poorly constructed or that have been badly implemented can result in long-term problems once the project has been completed.

No matter what the project is designed to achieve, the possibility of it failing is not insignificant. Some of the most common reasons for failure include:

- insufficient user involvement;

- lack of senior management/executive support;

- ambiguous requirements – either poorly articulated, poorly captured, or just plain incomplete;

- poor up-front planning;

- planning to catch up;

Smart voices: Apache helicopters[8]

Sometimes a project can run to schedule and still lead to problems. The British army's new fleet of Apache attack helicopters was delivered on time and to the project's original £3 billion budget. However, the training element of the project, which was procured under the government's Private Finance Initiative, is running three years behind schedule. This will mean that dozens of aircraft will have to be mothballed while the pilots are trained. The original timetable for training has been put back from April 2004 to February 2007, mainly because of the government's late decision to procure the training separately from the main contract, which resulted in the training contract being placed two years later (1998 instead of 1996). Storing the helicopters will cost an additional £6 million and the army will face problems because it has to scrap the anti-tank weapon that the Apache was meant to replace. Furthermore, there are now disputes with the supplier over the provision of spare parts, which may result in the Ministry of Defence cannibalizing parts from the mothballed aircraft.

- unrealistic expectations;

- no project ownership;

- unclear, unambiguous objectives, vision and goals;

- incompetent staff;

- unrealistic project expectations;

- inappropriate or non-existent risk management;

- severely compressed schedules – either imposed or overly optimistic;

- poor communication;

- inappropriate productivity expectations;

- generally poor project management; and

- concentration on the technological issues at the expense of the organizational.

One of the biggest risks within all major undertakings, and especially projects and programmes, is overcommitment, especially those that involve large capital expenditures or where people's reputations are at stake. Overcommitment or escalation refers to the inability to stop a major initiative, even when it is failing. The smart organizations should recognize the warning signs and act accordingly, or they might end up spending vast amounts of money on a project that delivers them nothing but a large hole in their accounts.

This type of problem is not just restricted to projects as it is often found in investment banks, when traders try to trade their way out of a loss. Many find it difficult to take a loss and instead hang on to losers. The problem is that a loss of 10 per cent requires a gain of more than 11 per cent to get even and a loss of 50 per cent requires a gain of 100 per cent. Therefore, without some kind of risk management mechanism, such problems can, in extreme cases, lead to the failure of an entire bank, as we saw with Nick Leeson and Barings. Similarly, without the effective management of risk within any project, failure can be a very real outcome. See Chapter 7 for more on decision making, overcommitment and decision support tools and techniques.

Operational risk

Operational risk has become a catch-all for a variety of risks that relate to the operations of the business. These tend to focus on the failure of the day-to-day controls and processes on which the business depends and cover such things as health and safety, internal sabotage (such as

Smart quotes

Operational risk management failures can significantly disrupt the quality and continuity of a firm's business activities. They may cause losses to the firm's clients or to the firm itself and at the extreme may cause it to become insolvent.

Financial Services Association

fraud), and security and controls associated with information systems. A good definition of operational risk is as follows: *the risk of loss resulting from inadequate or failed internal processes, people and systems.* The key thing about operational risk that separates it from many of the other risks the enterprise will face is that it exists in the natural course of corporate activity.[9] According to PricewaterhouseCoopers, the scope of operational risk management at the highest level can be broken down into two main components, which are themselves highly interdependent:

- Operational integrity, which is associated with the adequacy of operational controls and corporate governance. This encompasses the organization's culture, management supervision, errors, fraud, health and safety, compliance, physical disasters and poor internal controls.

- Service delivery, which relates to the organization's ability to perform business processes on an ongoing basis. This includes processes, IT systems, change projects, supplier relationships, personnel and crises.

The impacts of not managing operational risk can go far beyond the purely financial, which although damaging is never quite as catastrophic as a loss of reputation, for example (see section on 'Reputational risk', pp. 85–90). If you think about any organization, even your own, there is always a risk of an operational breakdown. With complexity increasing, the ability to manage every operational risk becomes all the more difficult. Therefore, just as operational risks can arise from a variety of sources, so too must the risk assessment. Sources such as internal audit, external audit, legal opinion, project risk reports, system availability reports etc. should be used to gain a clear understanding of what types of operational risks might be present.

In many respects operational risk management lies at the heart of many other of the risk categories. For example, the lack of operational controls allowed Nick Leeson to bring down Barings, and the actions of a small number of auditors ensured Andersen went to the wall. This sums up the nature of operational risk. Seemingly small and possibly innocuous actions can have major consequences. Operational risk often plays second fiddle to the larger risks that occupy the board and senior executives, such as strategic, financial and perhaps environmental risk. Indeed, a number of surveys on operational risk have raised a variety of barriers to its effective introduction to the corporate arena, including:

- no consistent definition;

- too much emphasis on the downside of risk;

- unclear and non-existent reporting lines, plus associated roles and responsibilities;

- no documentation; and

- misalignment with the organization's culture.

It is clear from the above that establishing an effective process for identifying and managing operational risks is not easy. It is no wonder, then, that organizations focus on the bigger risks to the detriment of

Smart things to say about risk management

They may seem unimportant or insignificant when compared to strategic risks, but operational risks can have dramatic consequences.

those that are considered less important. But organizations would be foolish to ignore their operational risks, given that they too have the ability to bring down a company.

Environmental risk

Smart quotes

What kind of state is the world really in? Optimists proclaim the end of history with the best of all possible worlds at hand, whereas pessimists see a world in decline and find doomsday lurking around the corner. Getting the state of the world right is important because it defines humanity's problems and shows us where our actions are most needed.

Bjørn Lomborg

The environment is fast becoming a major concern for everyone. The impact of human activity on the world's climate as well as local ecosystems is increasingly worrying and something that organizations can no longer ignore. Irrespective of the debates that might rage between the environmentalists and big business, there are plenty of examples of major environmental damage caused by the effects of commercial, governmental and military activity, including:

- Three Mile Island. The accident at the Three Mile Island Unit 2 (TMI-2) nuclear power plant near Middletown, Pennsylvania, on 28 March 1979 was the most serious in US commercial nuclear power plant operating history, even though it led to no deaths or injuries to plant workers or members of the nearby community. But it brought about sweeping changes involving emergency response planning, reactor operator training, human factors engineering, radiation protection, and many other areas of nuclear power plant operations. It also caused the US Nuclear Regulatory Commission (NRC) to tighten and heighten its regulatory oversight. Resultant changes in the nuclear power industry and at the NRC had the effect of enhancing safety.

- The meltdown of the nuclear power station at Chernobyl, Ukraine, in the former USSR. The accident destroyed the reactor and released massive amounts of radioactivity into the environment. After the accident, access to a 30-kilometre radius around the plant was prohibited, except for persons requiring official access to the plant and to the immediate area. The evacuated population numbered approximately 135,000. Pripyat, the town near Chernobyl where most of the workers at the plant lived before the 1986 accident, was evacuated several days after the accident because of radiological contamination. It was included in the 30-kilometre exclusion zone around the plant and is closed to all but those with authorized access. Thirty-one people died in the Chernobyl accident and its immediate aftermath, most in fighting the fires that ensued. The longer-term impacts on health linger on.

- The disaster at Union Carbide of India's pesticide plant at Bhopal. This occurred when a tank leaked poisonous methyl isocyanate gas into the atmosphere. Authorities said at the time it was the worst industrial accident in history, killing more than 3000 people and permanently injuring tens of thousands. Victims groups now put the fatality toll as high as 6000. Bhopal is a city faced with a health-care crisis. Struggling to deal with the aftermath of a 27-tonne leak of deadly MIC gas 18 years ago, an estimated 150,000 people are currently living with long-term gas-related health problems.

- The poor disposal of nuclear (military and non-military) waste in Russia. For example, the radiation levels at the Kola Peninsula, where there are 95 reactor cores with 35 tons of fuel from the Soviet Union's nuclear-powered submarine fleet, is thousands of times above normal.[10]

- *Exxon Valdez*, which leaked 11 million gallons of fuel oil into Alaska's William Prince Sound in 1989. This was responsible for killing 30,000 birds and contaminating hundreds of miles of coastline.

There is also increasing evidence that the world is heating up, with 2002 being the second warmest year since records began. Projections now suggest that the world's average temperature will increase between 1.4 and 5.8 degrees Celsius this century. Although this will have some benefits, such as the opening up of the Northwest Passage as the Artic ice sheet disappears around 2080, and a general reduction in respiratory diseases that come with cold weather, increasing temperatures are predicted to bring more extreme weather conditions, such as prolonged heat waves, severe storms, drought and flooding.

Big corporations – and especially those that affect the environment either directly through the extraction of oil, gas and ore or indirectly as a result of their activities such as the chemical, manufacturing and pharmaceutical industries – are literally cleaning up their act. These and many others are coming under increasing scrutiny from investors and regulators to keep pollution and possible environmental damage to an absolute minimum. A large number now produce non-financial reports that detail their approach to such things as the environment and how they minimize the environmental risks their activities raise.

Apart from the environmental impact, these reports cover two other dimensions that fall under corporate social responsibility (CSR), namely the organization's social and economic impact on those in society that it touches. Those organizations that take CSR reporting seriously take

Smart voices: The *Prestige* oil tanker[11]

On 19 November 2002, the oil tanker *Prestige* broke up in the Atlantic Ocean near the Spanish coast. The tanker, which was carrying 20 million gallons of fuel oil, broke up in storms 60 miles off Galicia. The ageing tanker began spilling oil at 08:00 and by late afternoon it had sunk. The leak spells disaster for the Spanish fishing industry, and hundreds of miles of coastline have been blackened by the oil. The ship was old and single-hulled, despite the recommendations following the *Braer* disaster in the Shetlands that all dangerous cargoes should be transported in double-hulled ships. It had also been cited twice for safety violations in the past. The long-term effect of the spillage will take years to assess and the recovery of the local environment and the economy will take a long, long time. Thousands of fish will die, which will impact marine life further up the food chain, such as seals and otters. The cost of the clean-up will run into billions.

the trouble to collect large amounts of information that pertains to the effects its operations have. A decade ago only a few dozen corporations produced such reports; today several thousand take the trouble to go to print, a clear indication of how public opinion about the environment has altered their behaviour.

Smart people to have on your side: Sustainability

- CSR consultancy and think-tank
- Benchmarks the CSR performance of corporations across the world
- Uses 49 criteria to assess each company in order to determine commitment to sustainable development
- Classifies each company according to the following five-point scale:
  1 truant
  2 cosmetic
  3 nerd
  4 virtuoso
  5 supersonic.

Technological risk

Smart quotes

Information technology and other new technologies have provoked profound structural changes in the world economy, and these are concocting unimaginable levels of complexity.

Ian Angell

As organizations have turned to technology in greater numbers, the levels of dependency have risen sharply. Dependence would not be an issue if the technology worked as expected, but technology is not that predictable. Its complexity makes it systemically unstable and, as a result, organizations can find themselves tied up in knots when it fails. For example:

- Incompatibility between the computers in Scotland's schools and the new Scottish Qualifications Authority's system led to delays and errors in students' results.

- The UK Passport Agency hoped that computerizing its offices would reduce the time and unit costs associated with processing passport applications. However, software glitches, and a higher than expected demand for child passports, led to such a severe backlog during the summer of 1999 that the Deputy Prime Minister had to intervene to resolve the problem. The cost of the additional measures taken by the Passport Agency to resolve the problems was around £12.6 million, and the unit cost of producing a passport for the year 1999/2000 was between £15 and £15.50, much higher than the £12 promised in the business case.

- Problems with the UK's Department of Social Security's (now Department for Work and Pensions) national insurance system (NIRS2) resulted in benefit claimants not receiving the money they were entitled to.

- In August 2002 the low-cost airline easyJet was forced to abandon its new rostering system and revert back to its old processes because the new system was inadequately tested before it went live and pilots raised concerns over its capabilities.[12]

- After ten years in development the UK's new air traffic control system has turned the country's airspace into the bottleneck of Europe. The project, which started in 1991, was plagued by software problems and when it was opened in January 2002 it was five years late and £180 million over budget. The new system has failed to live up to its performance expectations and the UK is now responsible for more air traffic delays than 30 other countries put together. The most serious problems have been caused by computer bugs and failures, which have led to cancellations and delays, which in turn have inconvenienced thousands of passengers.

- Florida's Children and Family Services Department child welfare system, which was designed to replace six legacy databases and manual records, has been plagued by politics, poor project management and changes to the system's functionality and architecture. The project started in 1994 and will now come into service in 2005, some five times over budget.

- A £130 million system for the coding of medical terminology, itself an essential building block for electronic patient records, was strongly criticized by a panel of 40 clinicians who found more than 800 faults. The problems with the system, called Snomed (Systematized Nomenclature of Medicine), included inaccuracies, missing data and duplication, as well as a heavy dose of political correctness, which prevented paediatricians from entering terms such as idiot, cretin and mongol.[13]

● The £10 million Globus system, developed by the Bank of England to process payments between institutions, has been troubled since its launch on 28 July 2003. The Bank has been forced to apologize and offer compensation after the system caused delays on large payments to financial institutions, government departments and foreign central banks. The problems have embarrassed the Bank, which is expected to provide failsafe operations.[14]

Smart voices: Imperial Chemical Industries (ICI)[15]

ICI recently joined many other companies whose operations have suffered significant disruptions following the introduction of new computer systems. Having spent a vast amount on installing a new supply management system at Quest, its Netherlands-based flavours and fragrances business, it is still struggling with a software problem that has disrupted supplies to some customers. As a result, many customers were sufficiently dissatisfied to take the opportunity to shift their business to ICI's competitors.

These are just a few of the many examples of both how we look to technology as a way of enhancing our business and what can happen when it fails to live up to expectations. There are of course literally thousands of computer glitches, failures and problems that occur every day, mainly while we are at work. Computers hang and crash and we lose our work and data. We also lose time because once our computers go down there is little else that we can do because our major work-based activities and functions normally involve computers of one kind or another.

If we think more widely, we can identify other areas of our lives that require us to depend on technology. Aircraft are increasingly controlled by computers, as are cars. The air traffic control systems on which the busy skies are managed are totally reliant on computer technology. Much of our health systems and retail distribution also rely on corporate IT systems. Dependence on technology is not a problem per se, but when it goes wrong it brings the scale of the dependency into sharp relief. This dependence raises some interesting risks, but not just those associated with dependency. Because technology encompasses a much wider range of business activities, risks can extend well beyond the organization. This is particularly true of the electronic channel which, although it has opened up a significant route to market, does represent new forms of risks. The types of technological risks that organizations need to guard against are detailed below.

Online fraud

Although it is difficult to assess the full extend of Internet fraud, it is believed that it represents approximately 0.9 per cent of online transactions. The costs to the merchant can be significant and are not just related to the loss of the goods secured fraudulently. According to ClearCommerce, costs fall into five areas, as follows:[16]

1   Cost of goods sold. As it will be unlikely that any goods will be recovered in the case of fraud, their value has to be written off. The

impact will be greatest for low-margin merchants. And, as a large percentage of e-commerce sites are low margin (because they have to undercut high-street prices to tempt people away from their bricks-and-mortar equivalent), this affects most sites.

2   Shipping costs. Fraudsters usually ask for high-priority shipping, as this allows them to complete their transaction as quickly as possible and avoid detection. And because shipping is usually bundled in with the order price, this too will have to be written off.

3   Card association fee. Card issuers such as Visa and MasterCard penalize merchants for generating excessive charge-backs. If a merchant exceeds charge-back rates for any three-month period, they are penalized with a $25 fee for every charge-back. And this fee increases up to $100 if the level is not controlled by the merchant in the following months. Those with excessive charge-back can be fined between $5500 and $100,000 per month and, in extreme cases, the card issuer will terminate the service agreement, thereby preventing the merchant from conducting business over the Internet.

4   Bank fees. Banks charge processing fees ranging from $10 to $25 for every charge-back.

5   Administration costs. On average, each charge-back requires up to two hours of administration.

Many online traders underestimate the level of fraud they can experience, especially when they are setting up their websites. Because fraud increases with the level of traffic, newly formed web merchants tend to ignore the importance of security and pay a heavy price.

Security breaches

The risks associated with the electronic channel are not restricted to Internet merchants, as any organization that is connected to the Internet is at risk from hackers and criminals accessing their systems. According to a 1998 PricewaterhouseCoopers and *Information Week* security survey of over 1600 management information systems officials from over 40 countries, nearly 73 per cent had experienced security breaches. Some had lost $10 million or more in single incidents.[17]

For some organizations, it is the number of breaches themselves that is an even bigger concern. A study by War Room Research suggested that more than 50 per cent of the companies they surveyed had experienced more than 30 system penetrations during a 12-month period and 60 per cent reported losing $200,000 or more from each intrusion.[18]

The impacts of viruses should also not be underestimated. For example, the Code Red virus defaced web pages, disrupted email, hampered online commerce and even forced computers to dial up the White House. The virus began replicating on 19 July 2001 and within nine hours had infected 250,000 systems. In response, the Pentagon shut down computer systems to assess its vulnerability and Microsoft had to issue a patch to its Windows 2000 and Windows NT operating systems to block the worm virus. The cost to businesses around the world ran into billions.

The latest piece of malicious code to hit the headlines comes by the name of 'Migmaf', a Trojan horse that goes around turning people's computers into servers that deliver pornographic ads on behalf of its creators. Basically the hijacked computers become a front, helping the true pornographers hide their tracks by concealing their real web address.

Businesses also have to contend with spam emails, which is the electronic equivalent of junk mail. Spam now accounts for more than half of all emails and the fight against it is expected to cost US businesses up to $20 billion in 2003. This issue has become so severe for Amazon, the online bookseller, that it has filed lawsuits against those it believes are responsible for the spamming.[19] The economic damage from malware (viruses, worms and other malicious computer code) cannot be underestimated. Table 2.1 gives the top ten viruses in terms of their costs, as estimated by mi2g, a UK digital risk management company.

The threats posed by the electronic channel are, of course, not always external. Disgruntled employees can wreak enormous damage when they hack into computer systems, plant viruses and delete essential corporate data. This type of risk tends to rise during economic downturns, when staff lose their jobs. For example, a 56-year-old systems administrator fired from his $186,000 job at a New Jersey chemical

Table 2.1 Economic damage caused by computer viruses

Virus	Cost ($ billion)
Sobig	27.8–34.0
Klez	13.4–16.3
Love Bug	7.8–9.6
Yaha	6.6–8.1
BugBear	2.4–2.9
Code Red	2.4–2.9
SirCam	2.0–2.5
MafiaBoy	1.0–1.3
Melissa	0.9–1.2
Slammer	0.9–1.1

Smart voices: The Slammer virus

The Slammer virus was one of the most virulent viruses to hit the Internet over the last 18 months and is believed to have cost global businesses in excess of $1 billion. The virus originated somewhere in South Korea in late January 2003 and within hours had affected more than 100,000 databases around the world. The virus found its way into a database running a Microsoft application and before long a deluge of messages swamped corporate databases, slowing down legitimate network traffic. In the US, the virus led to the shutdown of 15,000 Bank of America ATMs.

firm admitted causing $20 million worth of damage.[20] The man concerned used another employee's password to tap into the company's computer system through an Internet connection in his home to delete critical inventory and personnel files. In another case, an IT expert was accused of planting a computer time bomb in his former employer's network that permanently erased the company's manufacturing program, causing $10 million in damage. According to the Federal Bureau of Investigation and the Company Security Institute, such attacks led to a loss of $378 million in 2000.

A recent survey points to the scale and reach of cybercrime:[21]

- Two-thirds of the respondents had experienced serious incidents in the past year including hacking, virus attacks and credit card fraud.

- The main threat comes from external hackers, former employees and organized crime.

With some 700 viruses created every year, just how secure are your systems?

- Current employees account for 11 per cent of all crimes.

- Only 32 per cent of companies believe that business-to-consumer transactions are safe, compared to 53 per cent of business-to-business transactions.

Loss of data and systems

Many organizations would be lost without the systems and data they use every day. Because we are all so dependent on technology, we have to take more care in safeguarding the systems and data on which we rely.

Investing in me-too technologies

This type of risk should still be at the front of most CEOs' minds, as the technological bubble was fuelled by the insane herd instinct of CEOs who were desperate to get a piece of the Emperor's new clothes. Organizations, along with venture capitalists, invested billions on websites and New Economy business ideas that were nothing more than tin-pot and ill-thought-out ventures. And it seems that lessons have not been learnt. According to the annual survey of FTSE 100 website home pages by Porter Research, many companies have wasted millions of pounds on useless redesigns of their corporate websites. The survey cites Schroders and Severn Trent, which revamped their websites only to make matters worse. The firms were ranked 26th and 37th respectively in 2002, but in 2003 they had dropped to 98th and 97th.

Degradation of data and information over time

Ironically, with so much information swilling around an organization this risk seems at odds with the level of investment, but it is in fact a very significant risk for those organizations that exist for more than 20 years.

Brand risk

Brands are an increasingly important part of any business's armoury because they are a source of competitive advantage and a short cut for the consumer when they are making choices about whose product or

Smart quotes

The United States, one of the most technically advanced nations on the planet, is poised to enter a second Dark Ages – a time when what we leave behind will be viewed as negligible compared to the previous centuries. Although the causes are very different from those that precipitated Europe's Dark Ages, we are gambling with the contributions of our most profound thinkers to the arts, science, medicine, and the insights we've gained through exploration of the sea and stars. It's important to note that this hypothesis isn't dependent on intense global warming, a wide-scale nuclear attack, an asteroid hitting the earth, a plague or invasion by a foreign power. Although any one of these events would certainly precipitate a profound change in our society, the projection of a second Dark Ages is based on the natural progression of systems and processes already in place.

Bryan Bergeron

service they will use. Companies take immense trouble to build their brands because it helps to differentiate them from their competitors. Without brands there would be little to distinguish one product or service from another, apart from price. We are all familiar with the major brands such as Coca-Cola, Nike, Ford, Starbucks and so on, as

Smart quotes

In today's super competitive marketplace, all it takes is one mistake to hand your business over to your competitors. And once gone, your chances of getting it back are very slim. What's worse is that there are not one or two but an entire army of competitors out there to take advantage of your misstep. It wasn't long ago when Levi's, AT&T, Crest, Xerox, and Firestone were all top of their game, dominating the market with hardly a threat in sight. What happened to undermine their standing, as well as those of other superbrands?

Jack Trout

well as some of the newer brands associated with the Internet and electronic commerce such as Amazon and Yahoo. According to Paul Stobart,[22] differentiation is the most important concept in the development of a powerful brand. This, along with the building blocks of the brand proposition (i.e. position and identity), helps to create a brand that consumers can relate to. But this is only the supply side of the equation, as creating a brand that is accepted within the wider marketplace requires the organization to consider the following:

- brand loyalty

- brand awareness

- brand associations

- its perceived quality.

Of these, it is the perceived quality that is of paramount importance in creating a consistent and acceptable brand image – brand value is created only if certain standards of performance are attained every time the buyer comes into contact with the organization's brand. As Tom Peters suggests, a brand is a short cut or sorting device.

What are you going to do to protect your brand?

Clearly, having spent a long time building up a brand, companies want to protect it and build on it. Having a resilient brand is very important, especially as it is likely to be under attack from competitors and the inevitable problems that occur from time to time, such as product failures, broken trust and so on. But brands can die over time as markets shift and consumers change their buying habits. The primary areas of brand risk are discussed below.

Assuming your brand is strong enough

Once a strong brand has been created it has to be maintained. However, one of the problems with having a strong brand and the market dominance it provides is that it can generate a belief that no other competitor has the ability to attack your market share and reduce your brand's value. It also reduces the chances of spotting new entrants to the market, which almost destroyed IBM (see 'Smart voices: IBM', p. 82). There are countless instances of companies that were market leaders but which somehow succumbed to the threat of new competition or one of their archrivals.

A good example of this is Sainsbury's, which had long dominated the food retailing market until Tesco managed to steal the march. Sainsbury's lost its market position and is currently in the process of trying to regain it. But once a market position is lost, it can take a long time for it to be recovered. Indeed, Sainsbury's has recently dropped to third place behind Asda and may even drop to fourth, once William Morrison has acquired Safeway.

Brand stretch

Brand stretch is usually associated with a company extending its products and services beyond those that it is already known for. There is nothing wrong with stretching, and hence exploiting, a brand, but there are inherent risks associated with it (see 'Smart voices: Easy Internet Café', p. 83). Consider the Virgin brand. This originated in retail music but now covers a multitude of products and services, including rail travel, cosmetics, airlines, financial services and mobile phones/ network services. The expansion of the brand has not been without risk, especially within travel-related businesses. Virgin Rail has been dogged by poor service and delays and the airline business has been troubled by battles with British Airways.

Smart voices: IBM[23]

In 1992 IBM was at a crossroads. Since its beginnings in the early twentieth century, IBM was known for its pioneering of computer technologies, initially with punched cards and then with the mainframe computer. IBM's market share of the computing market advanced to 30 per cent. During this time, the organization's culture had evolved into a cosy world of limited competition, the result of its runaway success. IBM staffers used to be well known for their black suits and white shirts. Little variation was allowed. However, the shift to UNIX and then to personal computing managed to catch IBM unawares. It failed to understand the full impact of personal computers on its customers and the wider business community, believing only scientists and students would use them. It also believed that personal computers would never challenge its business.

As a result, IBM allowed Microsoft to take control of the operating system and Intel to control the microprocessor. By 1993, IBM's revenues were plummeting. Income from mainframes had dropped from $13 billion in 1990 to less than $7 billion. In the first four months of 1993, profit had declined by $800 million. In order to address these issues, the new CEO, Louis Gerstner, sought to reduce costs by almost $9 billion, which involved reducing the headcount by 35,000. This was in addition to the 45,000 people that the previous CEO, John Akers, had dismissed. Gerstner also took action to revive the brand, which, despite the problems, was still strong. This involved changing the performance measurement system, shifting the company to becoming more service-oriented as opposed product-oriented and expand its offerings in its middleware portfolio (which it did by acquiring Lotus Development Corporation).

All of these actions have helped to rebuild and expand the IBM brand, which is a remarkable achievement given the sorry state it was in at the beginning of 1993. As well as being the largest IT services company in the world, it has leading positions in computer hardware, software, mobile PCs, semiconductors and data storage.

> ### Smart voices: Easy Internet Café[24]
>
> Stelios Haji-Ioannou's stretching of the Easy brand beyond the highly successful easyJet low-cost airline has cost £120 million. In particular, the venture into Internet cafés has cost £96 million since it was launched in 1999. The business has failed to generate the much hoped-for profits and has now undergone major restructuring to make the larger sites more profitable and launch smaller Internet cafés in other retail outlets. For the next year or so at least, the venture will continue to be supported.

In a similar but more restricted way, Tesco was able to enhance its brand significantly by venturing outside the normal retail domain on which it was built. So, although stretching a brand can impose risk, it can also generate significant rewards. However, the Virgin brand remains a strong one. It is interesting to note, however, that many of the companies that ventured beyond their core product and brand offerings during the 1990s are now returning back to the primary services on which their reputations were made.

Rebranding[25]

Rebranding and changing the names of products and companies is increasingly popular. Although some are the result of mergers and acquisitions, many are the result of research and analysis into what messages existing brands convey to the organization's customers. However, there are plenty of examples where changing the brand's name has had disastrous effects. For example, the UK Post Office spent millions rebranding itself and changing its name to Consignia to allow it to compete more effectively on the international stage, only to revert back after customers believed that it would lead to the closure of local post offices. It is now known as Royal Mail.

In a similar way, PricewaterhouseCoopers' consultancy arm was rebranded as Monday and was widely ridiculed in the process. This also cost many millions. Shortly after, it was purchased by IBM (leading to another variation on IBM's acronym – 'I've Bought Monday'). Other companies have also suffered. For example, when Kellogg's decided to rebrand its successful cereal Coco Pops to Choco Pops it failed to take its consumers into account; they rebelled, forcing Kellogg's into a U-turn. Similarly, when Coca-Cola launched New Coke and rebranded the original formula Coca-Cola Classic, they found that no one was interested in the new product.

Avoiding some of the risks associated with rebranding means recognizing that brands belong to consumers and not the company. Therefore, if you are considering rebranding, engage the consumers for their opinions. It is also essential for management to explain their reasoning behind the change and ensure the new brand actually means something. Fancy words like Consignia and Monday just don't cut it.

Smart people to have on your side: Jack Trout

President of the marketing company Trout & Partners and author of a number of books on marketing, including *Big Brands, Big Trouble*, Jack Trout has identified a large number of lessons that every brand manager needs to apply, including:

1 Beware of success.
2 Don't lose touch.
3 You can't predict the future.
4 Never forget what made you famous.
5 Never underestimate a bigger competitor.
6 When you've got the chance, become the next thing.
7 Focus is critical in a competitive world.
8 Differentiation is critical in a competitive world.
9 Number two has to stay on the attack.
10 Don't put money into a dying brand; put it on a new idea.
11 Generic brand names are never as good as real brand names.
12 A brand that is many things cannot be one thing.

Mimicking the competition

This is often a fatal mistake, because consumers/purchasers will tend to opt for the known brand above another. Second is nowhere, in such circumstances. Therefore, just because a competitor produces a product should not mean that you should too, as people will usually continue with the market leader. The same is true of mimicking a competitor's idea and trying to market it as a unique selling point for your products. People will still associate the idea with the other company. It is far better generating something new or enhancing your existing products. In this way you will save money and reduce the risks of product failure.

Reputational risk

Smart quotes

Reputation is a broad and far-reaching asset incorporating concepts such as corporate image, goodwill and brand equity. It is a compilation of views held by all of the firm's stakeholders – investors, clients, customers, employees, suppliers, partners, vendors, media, financial analysts, special interest groups, politicians, labour unions, shareholder activists and regulators. The growth of the global marketplace, as well as the consequences of instant information exchange, intensifies the critical importance of a firm's reputation.

Jim Kartalia

Organizations rely on their reputations for many different reasons, including:

● maintaining their market position and brand;

● establishing productive working relationships with their suppliers;

Smart voices: British Telecom[26]

British Telecom has forced Sony to change one of its best-selling games because it shows a BT engineer shooting police. The game concerned is *Getaway*, which cost over $5 million to create and involves one mission that requires the player to steal a BT van and then, dressed as a BT engineer, attack a police station. BT believes the game has damaged its image and it may incite attacks on its employees.

- maintaining share price and ideally helping to increase it; and

- attracting and retaining talent (see also 'Talent risk' pp. 91–93).

No wonder, then, that they are fiercely protective when it is put at risk, but many do not do enough to either protect it or indeed shore it up during a crisis. The various sources of risk within a business, such as operational, financial, environmental and so on, can all impact a corporation's reputation. And, of course, there are the external sources, including consumer pressure groups, non-government organizations (NGOs), hackers (within the electronic space) and competition. This is particularly the case for multinational companies operating in developing countries and at risk from pressure groups and boycotts that can seriously hit their bottom line and do untold damage to their reputation. For example:[27]

- In September 2000, protestors from the Campaign to Eliminate Conflict Diamonds set up pickets outside Cartier on 5th Avenue, New York. Shoppers were confronted by images from the civil war in Sierra Leone with captions such as 'Did your diamonds do this?' The demonstration was reinforced by primetime television adverts aimed at forcing the US diamond industry to support legislation to stem the flow of illegal diamonds, thereby eliminating one of the major sources of rebel funds. Within eight months the industry agreed to block the import of diamonds coming from war zones. The response from the jewellery business was vital if it was to preserve the image and integrity of the diamond as a symbol of love.

- In 2000, the William Casey Institute led a successful campaign to persuade investors from an initial public offering by Petro-China, the Chinese oil company that was active in Tibet and Sudan.

- In 1999, Home Depot, the world's largest retailer of timber products, agreed to stop buying wood cut from old-growth forests after the Rainforest Action Network and other environmental groups held a series of protests in front of their stores and ran an advertising campaign that denounced the company.

A positive reputation is worth around one year's turnover.

Management Today

Similar actions have impacted other global organizations including Nike, Wal-Mart, Gap and Shell. And behind many of these actions are NGOs that have emerged to fill the void left by governments as they withdrew from setting the boundaries of corporate social responsibility. These organizations, which include Greenpeace and Amnesty International, have expanded in number and breadth over the last 20 years. There are now some 16,000 internationally recognized NGOs and a further 50,000 local equivalents operating in the developing nations.

The continued rise in NGOs means that organizations have to manage the risks from political, environmental, anti-capitalist and human rights activists as carefully as any other risks they face. In extreme cases these groups can cause major disruption, as we have witnessed with the anti-capitalist demonstrations and riots that have coincided with the Group of 8 (the eight richest nations in the world) economic summits around the world. This pressure for more business and social responsibility often focuses around single issues and usually blows up very quickly once it captures the public's imagination. The fact that it takes corporations by surprise demonstrates the limited attention they pay to this type of risk.

Service-based companies are probably more vulnerable to reputational risk than product-based organizations. This is because such companies have more to offer in terms of other products that are often branded separately to avoid risk by association. Therefore, when a product fails or is withdrawn from the supermarket shelves because of a health scare, the company that sells them does not go bust. Think of Perrier Water, the Ford Pinto and Persil Colour. All suffered major setbacks and were withdrawn, but the companies behind them did not fail. Product-based companies also tend to use multiple rather than single brands. This means that any problems with one rarely affect another because consumers are generally unaware that they are related. Also, responding quickly and openly during a crisis usually helps the business to recover as it reinforces the brand.

Unfortunately, when it comes to pure service-based organizations, which can rely only on the trust generated by their staff, the same does not apply. When trust is broken it is almost impossible to undo the damage. The demise of Andersen is probably the most extreme example of how dramatic this can be and should be a lesson for us all. Most corporate reputation disasters are in fact avoidable, so long as senior executives are both warned of them and are willing to address them.

Do not undervalue reputation because it is difficult to quantify and measure.

There are other forms of reputational risk that companies have little control over, but still need to respond to and these are associated with criminal activity.[29] Criminals, it seems, have good taste, which can cause problems for the companies whose products they use. For example:

- On Easter Monday 2003, Jason Fearson was shot dead in the passenger seat of an Audi TT in central London, following a gunfight at a nightclub. The lead singer of the garage group So Solid Crew was falsely accused of the murder. However, the band members have

Smart voices: Andersen[28]

Following the end of the long-running dispute between Andersen Consulting and Arthur Andersen in the summer of 2000, the consulting arm of the business changed its name to Accenture, as it was no longer legally allowed to use the Andersen name. Also, Arthur Andersen dropped Arthur in an attempt to exploit the Andersen Consulting name, which had spent $7 billion building up its brand.

Everything was going well until the news about Enron hit the press. Enron, once the doyen of the stock market, began to unravel. In October 2001 it announced a $1.01 billion charge related to write-downs in investments and a reduction in shareholder equity by $1.2 billion. This was shortly followed by an investigation by the Securities and Exchange Commission (SEC). By late October Andersen was shredding Enron-related documents. Once the truth about Enron came to light the firm started to suffer, but its complete unravelling occurred once they were found guilty of obstruction of justice in June 2002. The SEC issued a statement that Andersen was no longer able to audit public companies in the US. By this time it had lost more than half of its employees and a large proportion of its audit clients. Soon afterwards, it lost the rest.

Many Andersen employees lost their jobs, and many were absorbed into the remaining audit firms. But the impact of the collapse of Andersen on the remaining Big Four audit firms has been significant. All are now under increasing scrutiny from regulators and clients alike and most have lost significant revenue streams as their ability to carry out advisory services has been severely restricted. Interestingly, Andersen was reportedly considering severing its ties with Enron a year before the scandal made the headlines, but decided the significant fees outweighed risk to the firm's reputation.

had more than their fair share of brushes with the law, having stood trial for attempted murder, drug-dealing and gun possession. Their association with Audi was not a good one. They used the brand in their promotional material and Audi itself lent them two Audi TTs for the Brit Awards.

- The pop band Beastie Boys set a precedent by wearing Volkswagen badges around their necks, which sparked a wave of thefts from cars around the country.

- Mitsubishi suffered when millions of ecstasy tablets bearing the corporation's three-diamond logo flooded the market.

- Clothing companies Ben Sherman and Fred Perry have always been the preferred uniform of neo-Nazis and skinheads.

Smart voices: Caterpillar[30]

Heavy equipment maker Caterpillar is trying to block the release of the Disney film *George of the Jungle II* because it believes the film could damage its reputation. The film, which is a kid's comedy, features George, an accident-prone Tarzan figure, trying to save the jungle from being destroyed by evil developers. Unfortunately, the developers use Caterpillar's equipment and throughout the film the company's logo is clearly on display. Caterpillar is concerned that the film will have a negative impact on children and could affect its children's products.

The examples above and the many others you may have read about require those affected to react swiftly and decisively if they are to limit the impact on their reputations. Therefore, a company's ability to deal with a crisis is one of the most important factors when considering the short- and long-term impacts on its reputation. A crisis on its own may not bring a company's reputation to its knees, but how it deals with it can. Therefore, any firm worth its salt will have developed a standard approach for dealing with its major stakeholders in the event of a crisis (see Chapter 4).

Talent risk

Smart quotes

One aspect is fairly clear: traditional loyalty to a company is a thing of the past. In its place self-interest will dominate. If an employer cannot be trusted to look out for an employee's welfare (can any employers promise that today?), then any self-respecting individual is going to look out for number one. If this means pursuing other job and career opportunities, so be it. Better to jump first than to be victimized by an unexpected lay-off.

Terrence Deal and Allan Kennedy

It might seem strange to include talent as one of the major risks that organizations need to concern themselves with but, increasingly, organizations are finding that their ability to innovate, compete and maintain operational efficiencies relies heavily on the capability of the staff they employ.

Talent risk first emerged during the height of the dotcom boom, when the economy was still expanding and major employers were losing staff to the new-technology start-ups. Golden hellos were not uncommon and staff (a firm's most important asset) were firmly in the driving seat. Similarly, so were the headhunters, who exploited the revolving doors between one employer and the next, often headhunting the people they had only recently placed. Once the economy burst and staff were sacked (a firm's most expendable asset), the war for talent seemed to go underground as cost-cutting and downsizing pushed talent off the board's agenda. However, according to business consultants McKinsey & Co.,[31] this is far from the truth, as organizations are still desperately short of the talent they need to drive growth and manage the complexities they face. In fact, McKinsey believes that the war for talent will last for another 20 years, and it cites three reasons for this:

- The irreversible shift from Industrial Age to Information Age, which is increasingly reliant on knowledge workers.

- The intensifying need for high-calibre managerial talent as globalization, deregulation and technological change place greater demands on the organization and manager alike. Organizations need talented individuals who can reconceive their business and inspire their people. The short supply of managerial talent will be exacerbated by the ageing of the population.

- The growing propensity to switch companies. Most staff members are loyal to themselves, not to their employers. They all recognize that they are expendable despite the hollow words that they are important to their firm. Those who know their own worth are prepared to move companies if the deal they are currently getting does not meet their expectations.

How are you going to keep hold of your top talent?

One could argue that the current bear market has given the employer the upper hand once again, but as the market recovers, the merry-go-round of staff leaving to join other companies will begin once again and the war for talent will be back on the corporate radar. But most are poor at managing the risks associated with a loss of talent. Few have effective and workable succession plans and few, it seems, can be really bothered about their talent at all. According to McKinsey:

- less than 20 per cent of companies bring highly talented individuals into their business;

- only 3 per cent develop people quickly and effectively;

- less than 10 per cent retain almost all of their high performers;

- around 3 per cent remove low performers; and

- just over 15 per cent know who their high performers are.

Can you afford to have your talent walk out the door?

Most companies are complacent and seem to be unconcerned about the degree of talent risk they face. Only when it is too late do they make a half-baked attempt to retain their best staff. By then, of course, it is too late. Therefore, like any risk, it is vital to assess it and manage it, not ignore it. This leads us neatly on to the final category of risk we will discuss in this chapter.

Personal risk

Smart answers to tough questions

Q. What are you doing to manage your personal risks?

A. Few of us consider our personal risks particularly well. Maybe it's because of the way we function as human beings, or perhaps it's because we look to others to manage our risks for us, such as our employers, the government or the health system. We also tend to live our lives in a bubble of invincibility in which we feel protected and safe. Once it is pricked, however, we feel vulnerable and unable to deal with even the simplest of day-to-day events. Watching people who have become unemployed or divorced, for example, can be very instructive to the casual observer. Such people struggle to come to terms with the event and attempt to explore what led to the loss of their job or marriage. Many recognize that there were many tiny events that, in hindsight, should have provided them with the warning signs that all was not well. Unlike the risks associated with organizational life, which are more dramatic, personal risks are generally more subtle and take much longer to mature.

Most of the risks we take are taken intuitively or without due regard to the consequences. However, there are those that we seek actively.

For example, people regularly jump out of planes, scuba dive, go caving and so on in the knowledge that any of these could result in death. This knowledge does not prevent them from undertaking such activities, which may be because of the effect of this bubble of invincibility and the way we perceive the risks as either being too remote, long term or something that will happen to someone else. For instance, the popularity of roller-coaster rides is in part due to their ability to place the rider in a risky and potentially lethal situation without the fatal outcome. As rides become more extreme we are able to take ourselves nearer to death but without (apart from the unlucky few) ever experiencing it. Computer technology has allowed some rides in the US to reach 400 feet high, allowing people to plummet towards the ground at speeds approaching terminal velocity.

In a similar way, we pursue the other areas of our lives with the same thoughtlessness, believing that our careers will somehow be looked after by our employer, our debts repaid by a lucky lottery win, our old age provided for by a generous government and our health maintained by an increasingly sophisticated health service. The problem with modern life is that we can be fooled into the belief that sophistication equates to a lowering of risk, which generates a false sense of security. It is only when we suffer a shock that we tend to act but, of course, this is too late, as the risk has matured and we are having to deal with the consequences.

Part of the problem is that many of our personal risks are long term in nature, which plays against our general short-termist approach to life. Some examples are discussed below.

Weight and health

Most Western nations are suffering from the health issues associated with increasing obesity. There has been a dramatic rise in the numbers of people who are either overweight or obese, which is already causing

Smart voices: The risks of new technology[32]

Third-generation technology not only imposes risks for the suppliers: individuals are at risk too. The following story appeared in the *Sunday Times*.

A married man was on a boys' night out in the West End of London. Towards the end of the evening, and very much worse for wear, the hapless chap and his mates ended up in a posh nightclub. While there he managed to get entwined with a very attractive young lady. Unfortunately he was spotted by a friend of his wife, who happened to be sporting the latest in 3G technology, replete with the ability to take photographs and email them. A short snap later and the offending image was winging its way to his wife. When he got home, oblivious to what had happened, he was confronted by his distraught wife plus photo. There was no chance of escaping this one.

One can only speculate what happened next, but I am sure it was unpleasant. Many nightclubs have banned the use of new-generation mobile phones for this very reason.

alarm in the health services in the US and UK and increasingly across continental Europe. There are over 1.1 billion obese people in the world and this number continues to grow. The impact on our longevity is significant and, when combined with smoking, this represents a major personal risk. According to researchers in Framingham, Massachusetts, who followed several people from 1948 (when they were between 30 and 40) until 1990 (when about half of them had died), being overweight cuts life expectancy by more than three years and being obese by seven. Overweight smokers fared even worse, with their lives being cut short by thirteen years.[33] So, although the numbers of smokers might be falling, the number of overweight people is increasing.

Employment

The majority of us pass through our working lives with little consideration of where we would like to end up, what career path we would like to choose, or how we can remain in employment over the course of a 30–40-year working life. Most people's careers are accidental and few actively consider what skills they might need to remain in continuous employment. The combined effect of globalization, technology, stiff competition and economic uncertainty is leading to job losses. For example, the current turmoil in the financial markets and the massive reductions in the staffing levels of major investment banks means that few who are sacked will ever work again, because the skills they possess are not transferable. Of course, there are the fortunate few who can afford to give up work; but the majority are unlikely to be high earners ever again. Similarly, the exporting of low-level call centre work to places such as India, where a well-educated and cheap workforce is available, is increasing. What is of a greater concern is that this shifting of work overseas is beginning to affect the white-collar worker, where the impacts will be just as severe.

Many people believe that their employers will be looking out for them, without noticing that the world has changed, and it continues to change. The result is that their skills degrade and their attractiveness to their employer fades. Only when they are asked to leave do they recognize that more should have been done to future-proof their careers through such things as lifelong learning.

Old age and pensions

The West is facing a growing pensions crisis. The combination of falling stock markets and the inability of governments to provide adequate pension cover for today's workers as they retire will result in mass poverty for those who have always believed that they don't have to worry. Many have failed to save as much as they need to ensure that they

Smart quotes

Many a man with the chemistry of a great ballet dancer spends his time dancing with other people's dishes in a lunchroom, and others with genes of a mathematician pass their days juggling other people's papers in the back room of a bank or bookie joint. But within his chemical limitations, whatever they are, each man has enormous possibilities for determining his own fate.

Eric Berne

have a reasonable income when they retire. When they do realize, it is usually too late, as a healthy pension return depends on long-term investing. For example, a large proportion of the 11.1 million people in the UK who will reach pensionable age in 2014 show no sign of financial planning. This is particularly true of women, of whom barely 50 per cent have made provision.[34]

Governments will struggle to provide even the most basic of safety nets as the number of employed is outweighed by the pensioners they are meant to support. As a result, there is talk of raising the age at which people become eligible for their pension to 70. The joy of looking forward to an early retirement filled with travel and leisure has disappeared for all but those who have been prepared to invest early and make sufficient sacrifices to provide for their future. For the rest it's a frugal retirement or working until you literally drop dead. This, of course, is not just a UK phenomenon. In France, for example, there have been national strikes in response to the government increasing the retirement age for public sector workers. We have not heard the last of the pensions time bomb.

Workplace stress[35]

There is currently an epidemic of stress within the working population. Indeed, the number of employees claiming to have stress-related illnesses has tripled since it was last measured in 1996. In the UK, the number of days off sick due to occupational illness has risen from 18 million to over 33 million over the last five years, with the majority due to a relatively small number of employees taking more than six months off due to stress. The increasing intensification of work due to the impacts of technology and globalization, brutal, unforgiving employers, increased economic uncertainty and indebtedness all have their part to play. It's no wonder people are becoming more concerned about work–life balance.

Personal finance

On our death-beds, how many of us would say that we wished we had spent more time at work?

According to new research from the Prudential, around 15 million people could be suffering a wide range of physical, emotional, personal and professional problems as a result of their extraordinary ability to bury their heads in the sand when it comes to facing up to their financial concerns. A refusal to carry out even the most basic financial planning results in all sorts of problems. Nearly 7 million people admit to having sleeping problems, while more than 2 million say they're turning to drink. On top of that, more than 4.5 million have relationship problems, while the same number suffer from various forms of anxiety attacks and depression or an inability to concentrate at work. More than 3 million turn to comfort spending to avoid facing up to their financial worries – with the inevitable increase in debt.[36]

This chapter has covered a lot of ground and introduced many of the risks that an organization is likely to face. What I have not done is discuss each category in immense detail, because to do so would have meant writing a book on each. The purpose of this chapter has been to sensitize you to the types of risk you might meet, which I believe is fundamental to smart risk management. It should be clear, having read the chapter, that many of these are closely related, which makes their separation somewhat harder. I have also introduced a number of personal risks that all of us are likely to face at some stage in our lives.

Smart voices: Stolen identities[37]

The risk of having your identity stolen has tripled over the last three years. 2002 saw 40,000 cases of identity fraud compared to fewer than 13,000 cases in 2000. Fraudsters sift through people's bins, collecting information that can be used to prove identity. Bank statements, utility bills and similar documents contain valuable information about a person that can be used fraudulently. Other approaches involve obtaining the birth certificate of the victim, which requires no proof of identity, and then using this to join the electoral roll and obtain driving licences and so on. Many victims can run up debts mounting to many thousands of pounds without realizing it. With the risks of identity fraud rising, many people are buying personal shredders. It is now believed that stolen identities cost the UK economy £1 billion every year.

Understanding the nature of the risks that you may have to address is an essential building block to being able to manage them. But before you can do that, you must assess your risk appetite, as this will determine which risks you are willing to take and which you need to avoid.

Notes

1 See Crouhy, M., Galai, D. and Mark, R. (2001) *Risk Management*, New York: McGraw-Hill.

2 Meldrum, D. (2000) 'Country risk and foreign direct investment', *Business Economics*, January.

3 *MoneyWeek*, 16 May 2003, p. 5.

4 Gimbel, F. (2003) 'Investors ignore risky practices', *FT Fund Management*, 1 September, p. 1.

5 For a full exploration of Long-Term Capital Management, see Lowenstein, R. (2001) *When Genius Failed: The Rise and Fall of Long-Term Capital Management*, London: Fourth Estate.

6 Slywotzky, A., Quella, J. and Morrison, D. (2003) 'Countering strategic risk with pattern thinking: How to identify tomorrow's profit zones before the competition', *Mercer Management Journal*, No. 11 (sourced from www.mmc.com/views).

7 Marsh, P. (2003) 'The diligent dealmaker', *Financial Times*, 8 July, p. 13.

8 Odell, M. (2002) 'Helicopters grounded by delayed PFI pilot training', *Financial Times*, 31 October, p. 3.

9 Fortin, J. (2003) 'The road to BPM: Model, integrate, manage', in *Business Process: Integration, Workflow and Process Management*, London: Unicom, 24-25, June.

10 Jack, A. (2002) 'Russian nuclear rubbish tip challenges clean-up experts', *Financial Times*, 19 November, p. 20.

11 Millar, C. and Muir, H. (2002) 'Worst ever oil disaster', *Evening Standard*, 19 November, pp. 1–3.

12 Felsted, A. (2002) 'easyJet whips up a storm in the cockpit', *Financial Times*, 18 August, p. 10.

13 Hawkes, N. (2003) 'Doctors find £130m computer system unfit for work', *The Times*, 6 February, p. 11.

14 Swann, C. (2003) 'Bank of England apology for hitch', *Financial Times*, 21 August, p. 1.

15 Harris, C. (2003) 'Big questions for ICI posed by Quest unit', *Financial Times*, 26 March, p. 23.

16 ClearCommerce White Paper, *Fraud Prevention Guide*.

17 Boni, W. and Kovacich, G. (1999) *I-Way Robbery: Crime on the Internet*, Woburn, MA: Butterworth-Heinemann, p. 28.

18 Ibid. p. 28.

19 Harvey, F. and Morrison, S. (2003) 'Amazon lawsuits step up the fight against spam e-mails', *Financial Times*, 27 August, p. 1.

20 Alexander, G. (2001) 'Hacking by sacked staff costs US firms billions', *Sunday Times*, 5 August, p. 3.

21 Barker, T. (2001) 'Cybercrime is stifling e-business, warns CBI', *Financial Times*, 23 August.

22 Stobart, P. (2002) 'Creating powerful brands', in *Business, the Ultimate Resource*, London: Bloomsbury, pp. 62–93.

23 For a detailed analysis of IBM's rise, fall and rise, see Gerstner, L. (2002) *Who Says That Elephants Can't Dance? Inside IBM's Historic Turnaround*, London: HarperCollins.

24 Felsted, A. (2002) 'Easy Internet Café loses £80 million in two years', *Financial Times*, 23 December, p. 20.

25 Brooke, S. (2002) 'Pitfalls of rebranding', *Financial Times*, 3 October, p. 15.

26 Sherwin, A. (2003) 'Computer game is "insult" to BT image', *The Times*, 3 January, p. 8.

27 Alden, R (2001) 'Brands feel the impact as activists target customers', *Financial Times*, 18 July, p. 11.

28 For a detailed analysis of the fall of Enron and Andersen, see Fox, L. (2003) *Enron: The Rise and Fall*, Hoboken, New Jersey: John Wiley & Sons.

29 Braddock, K. (2003) 'When a brand becomes guilty by association', *Financial Times*, 17 July, p. 11.

30 *Metro* (2003) 'Disney's dig at digger cuts deep', 17 October, p. 3.

31 Michaels, E., Handfield-Jones, H. and Axelford, B. (2001) *The War for Talent*, Boston, MA: Harvard Business School Press.

32 Mills, S. (2003) 'Snappy messages can ruin your marriage', *Sunday Times News Review*, 6 April, p. 5.

33 Hawkes, N. (2003) 'Fat, forty and facing death', *The Times*, 7 January, p. 1.

34 Blitz, R. (2003) 'Ageing population trend heightens pension fears', *The Financial Times*, 30 January, p. 6.

35 Roberts, D. and Sherwood, B. (2002) 'Stressed workers give their employers a headache', *Financial Times*, 18 December, p. 3.

36 Mack, J. (2003) 'Don't be a financial ostrich', http://www.fool.co.uk/news/comment/2003.

37 Ungoed-Thomas, J. and Hamzic, E. (2003) 'Ministers to act on huge rise in stolen identities', *Sunday Times*, 5 January, p. 12.

38 Crouhy, M., Galai, D. and Mark, R. (2001) *Risk Management*, New York, McGraw-Hill.

3 Smart Thinking I: Know Your Risk Appetite

Killer question

What would you rather do – take calculated risks, or stagnate in a risk-averse corporate environment?

Attitude is a question of choice

As we saw in the previous chapter, organizations are faced with a variety of risks that must be adequately managed if they are to avoid financial loss. Navigating these risks is clearly important and is an essential skill, particularly at board level. But navigation is only part of the equation. Just as important is the ability to articulate the organization's risk appetite, as this defines how much risk it is willing to take and hence how much of a loss it might be prepared to suffer if things don't work out the way they were planned.

When things stop growing, they begin to die.

Charles Gow

Companies often fail to articulate their risk appetite well enough, which leads to two major problems – risk aversion, when they become too conservative, and cock-eyed optimism, when they become too opportunist. Both extremes result in problems in the medium to long term. For example, many companies expanded rapidly during the late 1990s boom only to find themselves paying the price of over-expansion following the bursting of the technology and investment bubble in early 2000. Another example involved the accountancy group Tenon losing £114 million as it expanded to become a contender to the Big Four accountancy firms (PricewaterhouseCoopers, Ernst & Young, KPMG, and Deloitte and Touche). Conversely, there are those organizations that have refused to take any risks at all, instead relying on the traditions that had made them successful in the past. Only when it is too late and they have lost market share or have become an acquisition target do they realize that conservatism was not the best approach to risk management. Indeed, an aversion to risk is currently pervading the business environment, itself a reaction to the increased regulation of organizations by government and the concern that big business is taking everyone for a ride and cannot be trusted. The combined effects of the Enron-type scandals, September 11th, economic downturn and the increased preference to pursue grievances through the courts has meant that most organizations are more concerned about not upsetting their stakeholders than taking risks.

Despite the current bias toward risk aversion, organizations must still be willing to take risks if they are to expand their market share. Standing still will ensure they stagnate as those among the competition that

Smart quotes

Living in a regime of irrational caution and restraint is already frustrating. Employees become frustrated because ethics departments, paranoid about the appearance of unethical behaviour, prevent them from doing normal activities. Managers of company divisions become frustrated when highly tedious doorstopper-like risk management manuals land with a thump on their desk, and they are asked to wade through them before making a decision. Trained engineers become frustrated when their firms refuse to do a radical innovation. Design consultancies become frustrated when their clients want every new idea to be researched to death in consumer focus groups. Caution and restraint will become more frustrating unless we challenge it.

Benjamin Hunt

are willing to take risks overtake them. And once the lead has been lost it can be very difficult to recover, as the retailer Sainsbury's is finding as it attempts to regain the number-one slot from Tesco.

A company can only take risks if the individuals within it are willing to take risks.

Risk, of course, is not all bad, as all the major advances in the economy – both in the past and now – have been the result of companies taking risk. Think of the Boeing 747, the railways, the Industrial Revolution, the creation of the personal computer and any other major innovation. In every case there was a desire to attempt something that had not been done before and take a risk. The key distinction, however, seems to be that when an organization chooses to take a risk it frames it as an opportunity, as innovation and as being entrepreneurial. So, although there is a risk that the venture may fail, risk-taking organizations are much more biased towards the positives than they would otherwise be (I will discuss innovation and its relationship towards risk in more detail in Chapter 8). They focus much less on the downside, although sometimes this is out of alignment with what happens (see 'Smart voices: JDS Uniphase', p. 106), and we should not forget the impacts of irrational thinking – believing that a positive outcome is almost guaranteed.

Conversely, when less inclined to exploit an opportunity, organizations will tend to emphasize the risks over and above the upside. In this case they look for reasons not to take a move outside their comfort zone. What is interesting about this, and indeed with respect to our general perception towards risk, is that it boils down to our attitude to risk taking and whether or not we believe the upside outweighs the downside. We all probably know, or have heard of, people and companies that have a much larger appetite for risk than others. For example, compare serial entrepreneurs, who will always rise from the ashes of a failed venture to start another, to someone who is unwilling even to change jobs because they fear the unknown. Attitude is therefore a key factor in the management of risk.

Fortune favours the brave.

Smart voices: JDS Uniphase[1]

In a little under a year, JDS Uniphase, the world's largest optical components manufacturer, went from rapid growth, in order to meet a massive upturn in demand, to announcing huge losses ($56.6 billion). The turnaround in fortunes has much to do with the excesses of the tech bubble that burst in 2000. But it is also associated with the management of risk. Write-downs of $44.8 billion in relation to the acquisition of various telecom companies over the previous two years were, according to some commentators, a 'massive mistake' and a 'huge waste of shareholder funds'. Although the acquisitions were paid for by JDS Uniphase shares, and hence the loss was only on paper, the company missed the opportunity to use these shares to purchase non-telecom companies that would have allowed them to weather the storm. In this case, the risk management approach did not match the company's risk appetite.

Attitude to risk is an individual trait

Attitude cannot be summed up in organizational terms, as it is fundamentally an individual trait that lies at the heart of how we behave when faced with a risk. If you asked a few people what they would prefer to do when faced with a choice of base-jumping off Angel Falls, scuba-diving in the Caribbean or relaxing on a beach with a good novel, you would expect them to respond differently. A very small proportion would love the prospect of hurling themselves off the top

Smart quotes

Corporate America has got to move on. I worry about the loss of risk-taking zeal. People are confusing risk taking with legal risk taking, which is a mistake.

William Donaldson

of Angel Falls; more, but still not a majority, would be happy to dive into the sea and swim with the fishes; the majority would probably prefer to sit on a beach with a good book. This suggests that most of us would rather not risk very much at all. This is reflected in organizations and society at large. There are very few entrepreneurs, but plenty of employees who look to those who take risks to help drive the business forward. So what is it that makes some people more willing to take risks than others? To answer that question we need to understand fear and some of the wiring in our brains that leads us to avoid situations that involve risk and failure.

Fear is a universal emotion that affects us all. It developed a long time ago to protect us against predators. The physiological response to fear is automatic. Adrenaline is pumped around our bodies to allow us to respond as quickly as possible to a perceived threat, and our brain does not allow us any time to consider our options before taking action – the amygdala (the ancient part of our brain that holds pre-programmed responses that have been with us for millennia) overrides the cortex (the modern part of our brain with which we reason). Although this response is critical to our survival if, say, we were faced with a ravenous tiger, it serves us badly in modern society where over-responding to novel or risky situations can cause all sorts of problems including stress, high blood pressure, heart disease and ulcers. Unfortunately we cannot override it because of its deep-seated nature. It also ensures that we fail to take many of the opportunities that present themselves throughout our lives.

The second component to our individual attitude to risk is related to our internal wiring. In a general sense, we are conditioned to seek out pleasure and avoid pain. Fear is an extreme case of this, but even a seemingly innocuous situation can provide enough of a concern about pain that we avoid it. For example, many of us – me included – find the prospect of entering a room full of strangers a daunting experience and one that we would rather avoid. In fact, we would rather be anywhere else. We feel anxious, tongue-tied and apprehensive, worried that we won't know what to say, that people won't like us and will think our small talk uninteresting and dull.

We have been conditioned to avoid anything that could lead to a painful outcome (however we define it). Therefore, because we frame a risk as something that has a negative outcome, we immediately start to do all we can to avoid it. In a similar way, if we have made a mistake, we would rather try to hide it than come clean because of the perceived or actual consequences. Everyone's lives have been shaped by what they have learned that gives them pleasure and what they have learned that gives them pain.[2] These are very powerful patterns. To overcome them and the associated risk aversion, every time you are faced with a situation that presents a risk, ask yourself these two questions:

1   What are the consequences of not taking action? – What will it cost me? What is the pain? How does the pain make me feel now?

2   What are the benefits of taking action? – What will I gain? What is the pleasure? How does it make me feel now?

Of course we probably know people who believe that risk taking is all about pleasure. They get their kicks by doing things which are out of the ordinary, such as extreme sports, driving very fast cars and so on – they have a live-fast, die-young attitude to life. They will never consider the consequences of the first question. For most of us, asking ourselves the two questions above is an excellent way to keep our natural risk aversion in check. Another way is to consider how you view risk, either as an opportunity or asset, or as a liability or danger. Your attitude will define how you will manage the risks you face, as illustrated in Table 3.1.

Risk is the enemy of constancy.

Although it is a matter of choice, many of us respond to our surroundings and the situations we face automatically. But we do have a choice, and spending a little time considering the options, the positives as well as the negatives of the situation and your response, is a great way to begin to take a calculated approach to risk. Attitude, after all, is a frame of mind.

Table 3.1   Attitudes and approaches to risk

Risk as an opportunity	Risk as a danger
Seeking out and taking opportunities	Avoiding and turning down opportunities
Increase the chances of gain	Reduce the possibility of loss
A chance to create value	A way of preventing value destruction
Lose control and embrace the unknown	Avoid the unknown and remain in control
An opportunity to stretch and learn	A chance to avoid appearing incompetent

Risk attitude within organizations

Risk appetite in organizations is, of course, different from the beliefs held by individuals. But organizations comprise many individuals,

Smart quotes

The problem with the enormous rise of risk management is that it entrenches a new intolerance of risk and uncertainty. So, before being allowed to take action, employees need authorization under new risk controls. Rather than take chances, managers feel they must filter every decision through elaborate risk assessment schemes. Companies now seek to hedge risks that in the past would have been accepted as business risks. Managers are now far more obsessed with the discipline of crisis management. Rather than just get on with it and take risks, and act on strong positive beliefs, more and more action is predicated on the fear of what might go wrong.

Benjamin Hunt

each with their own risk appetite. So the question we need to ask ourselves is: what is risk appetite and how can organizations articulate it well enough to make the appropriate judgements and decisions when faced with opportunities and, of course, risks?

According to PricewaterhouseCoopers, an organization's attitude to risk can be viewed along a continuum of increasing sophistication.[3] At the lowest end of the continuum organizations tend to manage risks on a reactive basis. The focus is principally on compliance and control as a means of protecting themselves from the downside risks. Avoidance is high on the agenda. Therefore, whenever a new risk appears they will seek to control it by enhancing their control environment.

For those organizations that can be considered to have a more mature attitude to risk, and as a consequence more sophistication, the focus is on trying to understand the full range of risks facing them. To do so requires an acceptance of a broader definition of risk that goes beyond the simplistic controls and financial loss of the unsophisticated organization. Such mid-attitude organizations evaluate operational, compliance and other types of risk and will generally seek to identify and apply best-

Smart voices: Canon[4]

When IBM attempted to take on Xerox in the copier business, it failed. But when Canon tried, it succeeded – by taking fewer risks than IBM. Canon did it by entering the copier business by licensing technology from foreign partners. It used borrowed technology and borrowed channels. More important to its success was its ability to learn at low cost about part of the copying market not served by Xerox. When Canon finally developed its alternative to Xerox's products, it licensed it to many of Xerox's competitors. The fees from its licensees helped Canon to fund its research and development activities and target its development approaches.

practice techniques, processes and governance structures. They also take an interest in what happens to their competitors and, where appropriate, will bolster their own risk management processes when they see a competitor's fail. The attitude to risk is therefore more balanced.

Finally, in enterprises that have the most sophisticated attitude to risk, opportunity is incorporated into their risk evaluation processes. They firmly believe that in order to improve their shareholder value they must be willing to take risks. Therefore, they take the trouble to evaluate the strategic and business risks they run in the pursuit of growth and innovation and build in suitable controls to manage them effectively. What is interesting about such companies is that they will deliberately seek to turn risky events into opportunities to create competitive advantage. This is achieved in two ways. First, by building risk into the decision-making process and, second, by building it into their decision-monitoring processes. The most sophisticated organizations have a comprehensive understanding of risk and ensure this is promulgated throughout the entire enterprise through a risk management framework that everyone can use. Most critical, however, is the role of senior management and especially the board, who provide the necessary risk leadership that allows everyone to take suitable risks without worrying about the consequences of failure (more on this in Chapter 5, when we talk about developing a risk culture).

The important thing about organizations at the 'sophisticated' end of the spectrum is that they view risk as an asset and do not spend all their time trying to minimize it. In the end, risk taking is all about reward and opportunity, rather than trying to avoid failure. Table 3.2 outlines the focus and outcomes at each level of sophistication.

Another way to look at how companies approach risk is to combine the attitude to risk with its management (Fig. 3.1). This leads to four types of behaviour, as follows:

Lemming

When the management of risk is poor and the attitude is one that deliberately seeks out risk, the behaviour can be considered to be the same as the lemming. In such instances the organization blindly follows a course of action without any understanding of the risks it is running. And, like the lemming, it will wind up at the bottom of a cliff. Examples of such herd-like behaviour can be found in every bubble since

Table 3.2　Organizational approaches to risk by level of sophistication

Sophistication	Focus	Outcomes
Low	Compliance and prevention	• Avoiding own organization's crises • Complying with corporate governance standards • Avoiding personal liability failure
Medium	Operating performance	• Understanding the full range of risks facing the business today • Understanding and evaluating business strategy risks • Achieving global best practice
High	Shareholder value enhancement	• Protecting the corporate reputation • Enhancing capital allocation • Improving returns through value-based management

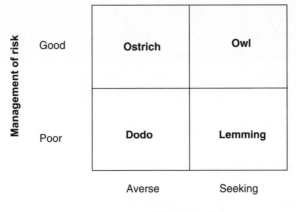

Fig. 3.1 Organizational classifications

Smart voices: Amey[5]

Shares in Amey plunged from over £4 to 25 pence over 2002 as the company suffered from its over-expansion into the private finance initiative. This cost the jobs of the chief executive and two finance directors. The company racked up losses of £129 million during the 2002 financial year after it had to allocate £110 million for restructuring charges, mostly relating to write-offs and write-downs.

the Tulip Bubble (see 'Smart people to have on your side: Charles P. Kindleberger', p. 115).

Dodo

When the management of risk is poor and the attitude to risk is averse, the organization can be likened to a dodo, destined for extinction. Not only are such organizations appalling at managing the risks they face, but they also avoid any opportunities for growth and innovation. These are the companies that wind up as an acquisition target, or fade away as their markets change and the competition chips away at their market share. For example, if you were to look at the Forbes Index of the top 100 industrial companies in 1917 (when it was set up) and compare this to the list in 1987, you would find the following:

- 61 companies had ceased to exist;

- 21 companies had left the top 100; and

- only 18 companies remained.

We can pretty much guarantee that the companies in 1917 didn't think that most of them would have gone bust or left the index within 70 years.

Ostrich

When the management of risk is good but the attitude towards it is averse, the organization can be classified as an ostrich. This is the organization that has become so good at managing risk that it is able to identify every possible problem, thereby negating the need for it to take any action that is considered remotely risky. Where it comes to the upside of risk and innovation, senior management have their heads buried in the sand and are unwilling to take them out again. Any innovation or opportunity that involves taking risks is given the stock answer – no.

Owl

When the management of risk is good and the attitude is one that seeks out risks (opportunities), the organization is more owl-like. In other words, and like the owl, it is able to scan the horizon for opportunities and intelligently weigh up the risks it faces. This category comprises the businesses that have achieved the right balance of taking educated risks backed up by best-in-class risk management processes.

Smart people to have on your side: Charles P. Kindleberger

Charles P. Kindleberger is an academic economist, a consultant to the US Treasury and Federal Reserve and the author of *Manias, Panics and Crashes*. He helped to draw up the Marshall Plan for American aid to Europe after World War II and believes that every financial crisis in history has followed the five stages below:

- *Speculation*. Events that lead up to a crash usually start with an outside shock, such as the end of a war, a revolutionary invention or some kind of unanticipated change in monetary policy. This leads to profits in some areas and losses in others. If the opportunity outweighs the losses, a boom begins.
- *Credit expansion*. As investors see the opportunity to make a fast profit, they all pile into the markets and entrepreneurs set up new companies to cash in on the boom. This is fuelled by the availability of money and credit and, before too long, euphoria. Investors fail to question the validity of their investment because they are more concerned about losing out on a fast buck.
- *Financial distress*. As the speculative boom continues, interest rates, velocity of circulation and prices begin to mount. Eventually, a few insiders decide to take their profits and cash in their investments. As a result, investors begin to hesitate and a period of financial distress ensues in which the investment begins to disappoint. Symptoms include demands on the capital market for cash when cash is difficult to get hold of, rising interest rates, increased bankruptcies and the deterioration of price rises. At this point you should expect to see the failure of a bank or financial misconduct of those at the core of the investment.
- *Panic*. This begins shortly after the financial distress stage, as more and more people withdraw from the investment and prices fall sharply. People begin to panic and everyone tries to sell.
- *Crash*. This selling continues until: prices fall to such low levels that people are tempted to start to invest again; trade is cut off by setting limits on price declines; or a lender of last resort (usually a central bank) succeeds in convincing the market that money will be made available to meet the demands for cash. The end point is normally signalled by revulsion – the point at which disillusioned investors refuse to participate in the market at all and prices fall to levels way below their true value.

Organizations determine their risk management appetite in a variety of ways, but whatever process is adopted, the underlying ethos should be to balance the various factors, both positive and negative. In the process they will typically ask themselves a number of questions, including:

- Is the risk consistent with the company's strategy and philosophy?

- How does it compare to its history of gains and losses?

- Is the organization's management capable and competent enough to manage the risks?

- Do all stakeholders, including external ones such as investors, understand the risks and why the business is taking them?

- How will the risk impact the business cashflow and balance sheet?

- How will the risk impact the operations of the business?

In addition to assessing an organization's appetite, the board must ensure that adequate capital is allocated to the primary risks the company is going to take, that the greater the risk, the greater the return, and that the most economic method of managing the risk is chosen. In this way the risk appetite of the organization can be matched to the investment required to manage it. Where these are out of alignment, you know you have got a problem.

Another way to ensure an organization's risk appetite is appropriate is to match it to where it sits along the organization's life cycle. It is well known that every organization follows a life cycle (see 'Smart people to have on your side: Ichek Adizes', p. 119) and at every stage there are risks that have to be managed in order to grow and expand. Although there are many risks associated with the early stages of an organization, such as those we witnessed with the dotcoms, it is the decline stage that presents the greatest risk of all. As the name suggests, the decline stage is when the company either goes to the wall, is sold or can somehow turn itself around by reinventing itself, in the way that IBM was able to do during the 1990s.

There are other problems associated with ageing companies that have been in existence for a long time, and this is associated with a general unwillingness to rock the boat. Maintaining the status quo is much simpler than taking risks. Collectively the organization falls into the same psychological traps as individuals and avoids anything that could cause it pain. It becomes much easier to go with the flow and assume that the stable business environment in which the organization exists will be maintained in perpetuity. This attitude ensures that innovation is kept in check and the enterprise's ability to transform itself and maintain competitiveness is severely hampered.

Although risk management is a complex and sometimes difficult process for stable organizations to deal with, managing risk when a business is in crisis is even harder and yet is all the more critical. According to Stuart Slatter and David Lovett, authors of *Corporate Turnaround*, there are 13 telltale signs that indicate whether an organization is in danger of failing. These are:

- poor management;

- inadequate financial control;

- poor working capital management;

- high costs;

- lack of marketing effort;

- overtrading;

- big, unwieldy projects;

- ineffective acquisitions;

- weak financial policy;

- organizational inertia and confusion;

- adverse changes in market demand;

- strong competition; and

- adverse movements in commodity prices.

In this chapter we have reviewed the importance of attitude to risk, both at the individual and organizational levels. Attitude is a significant driver of action. A positive attitude towards risk yields the belief that the greater the risk, the greater the opportunity. Organizations need to encourage a better and more positive attitude to risk and to do this they need to develop a risk culture, which is something that will be covered in Chapter 5. Before we can discuss this, we need to cover one important element to effective risk management: formalizing the process.

Smart people to have on your side: Ichek Adizes

Founder and director of the Adizes Institute in Los Angeles and author of *Corporate Lifecycles* and *Managing Corporate Lifecycles*, Ichek Adizes believes every organization has the capability of passing through a life cycle characterized by ten stages (five associated with growing and five with declining or ageing), as follows:

1   Courtship. This is characterized by the ideas and possibilities of the founder(s), but if the ideas are not followed through then the company can fail, leading to a fleeting affair, doomed from the start.
2   Infancy. Once established, the focus of the business changes to the production of results, but if the founder fails to delegate or fails to manage cashflow then the infant dies – infant mortality is therefore the biggest risk.
3   Go-go. Having survived infancy, most businesses then expand, turning their hand to everything they can. They are seemingly invincible and have a huge appetite for results, and growth. They can become exceptionally arrogant. But they have to beware the founder's trap, where the link between the founder and the company is inseparable, making it difficult for them to let go and establish the effective controls required to delegate effectively.
4   Adolescence. During this stage of the life cycle, the company is reborn as it finally departs from the legacy of the founder. In particular, it is characterized by the shift from entrepreneurship to professional management. As expected, this stage of the corporate life cycle involves a lot of conflict and can result in divorce, and so the company may never achieve its full potential.
5   Prime (early and late). This is the optimal position in the life cycle and usually precedes the declining phases. As it suggests, a company that is in its prime is typified by high performance, market leadership, a committed and effective workforce, and sound governance and decision-making structures. Organizations in their prime are mature and efficient businesses. The major problem enterprises have at this stage is continuing to operate at their prime. There is still the risk of divorce and the added risk of the fall, which is often associated with a loss of flexibility, itself born of complacency.

6 Fall. This is the tipping point for the company. No longer in its prime, it starts to exhibit all the signs of ageing, including a desire to avoid risks. Expectations start to exceed results and the company focuses on avoiding new opportunities; it begins to get personal, and seeking permission becomes a major focus; it tends to see problems, not opportunities; it allows inertia and politics to dominate.

7 Aristocracy. As with any aristocracy, this stage is typified by inaction, an aversion to change, an obsession with stability and tradition and a reduction in expectations. As a result, there is little or no innovation and both the internal and external stakeholders know that the company is in dire straits.

8 Salem City. Just like the Salem witch hunts, this stage of the life cycle is characterized by internal turf wars, power plays, the search for the cause of the decline and people who are terribly concerned about protecting themselves and attacking others. This is not a friendly place to be. Paranoia reigns as everyone knows that the business is in decline.

9 Bureaucracy. This is the clinically sustained organization. All the entrepreneurs have long since gone, leaving the administrators to run the business. Their major concern is rules, process, procedures and hierarchy and they are certainly not bothered with innovation, or serving the customer. The organization has become inward-facing and self-serving, with no viable future apart from that upheld by political indecision.

10 Death. This pretty much explains itself. This is normally defined as a lack of resources required to sustain the business. In other words, debt, expenditure and costs outweigh income. But many organizations die when no one remains committed to the organization and, in this case, it is a slow and painful process.

Adizes also suggests that as companies make the transition from one life-cycle stage to another, difficulties arise because they have to learn new patterns and abandon their old ones.

Notes

1   This case study is derived from an article that appeared in *Money Week*, 3 August 2001, p. 28.

2   Steele. J., Hiles, C. and Coburn, M. (1999) *Breakthrough to Peak Performance*, London: The Catalyst Group, pp. 121–36.

3   PricewaterhouseCoopers (2001), *Risk Management Forecast* 2001, pp. 11–12.

4   Hamel, G. and Prahalad, C.K. (1994) *Competing for the Future*, Boston, MA: Harvard Business School Press, p. 136.

5   Lea, R. (2003) 'Amey racks up £129 million loss as it counts cost of PFI', *Evening Standard*, p. 36.

4 Smart Thinking II: Formalize the Process

Smart quotes

The problem is that, in most companies, risk management is a silent partner. Everyone blindly assumes that risk management processes are producing a stability basic to the company's survival and prosperity.

PricewaterhouseCoopers

As regards risk management, understanding your risk appetite is merely the beginning of smart thinking. But, no matter how well this is articulated, without a formal process through which risks can be described, monitored and controlled, there will be plenty of surprises. Creating a formal process, which everyone can use, is therefore an essential undertaking.

It is important when developing and implementing such a process, that it meets the needs of the organization and does not override judgement. When it comes to risk management, many organizations suffer from the two extremes of process management. The first is that they have no process at all, which leads to the usual problems of inconsistency, poor decision making, errors, shocks and surprises and an ad hoc approach to the management of risk. The second, which can be equally dangerous, is when the process takes over. Here people spend enormous amounts of time and effort following the process rather than managing the risks. Formalizing the risk management process therefore must follow some simple guiding principles, including:

- The process must not be too onerous. If it is, people will not use it.

- Any scoring mechanisms must be simple and ideally based on an even, not an odd, scale (in other words, risks should be rated, say between 1 and 4, not 1 and 5). This avoids the temptation of always choosing the middle ground, which rarely helps the decision-making process; nor does it provide the opportunity to separate similar risks. In simple terms, there is regression to the mean.

- The scoring mechanism should not be precise. If it is, it will lead to unnecessary debates about what the numbers mean. The scoring mechanism should be used to guide judgement, not become a substitute for it. I have seen too many organizations obsess about the scoring of risks to the detriment of effective decision making.

- Risks must be manageable and within the remit of those charged with their management. Once again organizations fall into the trap of identifying risks that are outside their control. It is far better to have risks that are both understood and within the organization's capabilities to manage them.

- Ownership and accountability must be present, as without this no actions will be taken to manage the risks once identified. This is often one of the toughest nuts to crack, as people are generally more comfortable with identifying risks than being accountable for their management.

The basic risk management process

An effective risk management process (see Fig. 4.1) should consist of four basic processes – identify, quantify, respond and manage – supported by what I term the four pillars of risk management – define the risk framework, articulate the risk appetite, create a risk culture and establish a clear risk governance mechanism. Ultimately, the risk management process should be designed to aid both decision making and risk taking. If it fails on either count, the process has failed to deliver to its objectives.

Identify

The identification stage of the risk management process involves capturing those risks that might impact the enterprise and its principal ac-

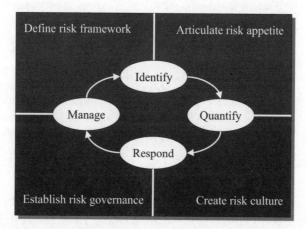

Fig. 4.1 The risk management process

Smart people to have on your side: Helga Drummond

As Professor of Decision Making at the University of Liverpool and author of *The Art of Decision Making*, Helga Drummond believes the art of decision making is knowing what questions to ask, and she provides the following advice to decision makers:

- Rise to the right level of events – match the response and application of judgement to the current situation, not past experiences.
- A dog is for life – make sure there is always a way out of a situation before you enter it, which includes quitting if necessary.
- Liars serving the truth – use information appropriately and in many cases sparingly; too much can distract you from making the right decisions.
- Take a walk on the wild side – seek out information from alternative sources, not just those that you are familiar with.
- There's a rumour going round – always an interesting and useful source of information.
- Opposites – where a decision is intuitively appealing, take great care.
- Look hard and look twice – test out your assumptions and keep these to a minimum.
- Quacks bawling – look for the political drivers behind decisions.
- Buying a 'cut and shut' – when everything appears too good to be true, check it out.
- Fortune favours the brave – think in second-order terms, not first-order. Whereas the latter involves approaching the decision from an existing framework, the former involves thinking more laterally and being prepared to think around the problem rather than directly at it.
- Escaping to reality – always engage in reality testing to remove lingering doubts.
- Creating luck – the art of decision making is to minimize risk.
- Time and tide – although planning and control are essential in decision making, success depends largely on being sensitive to changing circumstances.

tivities. Clearly, the types of risks that will be identified will depend on the context in which we are dealing. Thus, project-related risk would be different in nature, impact and timing to strategic risks. In addition,

> ### Smart quotes
>
> Organizations should try to avoid 'risk identification overload', as this can prevent the significant risks being given appropriate attention. If lots of risks have traditionally been identified, they can usefully be analysed on the basis of relevance to meeting the business objectives and to highlighting areas where new objectives may be needed.
>
> Anthony Carey

the process through which they might be identified might also differ. For example, project risks can be identified from a number of sources, including the plan, the product breakdown structure and stakeholder analysis. Strategic risks can be identified through scenario analysis, market analyses and an assessment of the organization's primary business drivers. Although the context may differ, there are a number of common techniques that can be used to identify risk, including:

- Structured thinking.

- Involvement of experts.

- Brainstorming.

- Analyses of past and other people's failures.

- Analysis of past and other people's successes.

- Checklists.

- Analysing critical success factors (which by their very nature must be achieved if the organization is to be successful).

- Testing and analysing assumptions. In the absence of total knowledge, we have no choice but to make assumptions about events that will take place in the future. Instead of expecting the assumption will hold true, change perspective and consider what would happen if it didn't. In this way it is possible to switch an assumption into a risk.

- Using the potential sources of risk as a way of identifying them. This could include technical, environmental, people-based and so on. In fact, if the organization has defined its risk framework (one of the four pillars), many of the sources will have already been captured, which will make the identification of risk easier.

I discuss a small number of the techniques, tools and models of risk management in Chapter 7.

Smart voices: The New Zealand Government[1]

In New Zealand, risk-based funding rules for complex projects have been developed. Using quantitative risk analysis, each risk is assessed along with its impact and probability. Thus, the fiscal impact of a project's risks can be made explicit to decision makers.

Quantify

Having identified the risks, the next stage is to quantify them. Risks are typically quantified along two dimensions:

1   Impact. This is usually measured in terms of financial consequences (loss), either in terms of the bottom line, market share, loss of sales revenue or impact on share value. Whatever measure is adopted, it should indicate the types of loss expected if the risk matures. When it comes to projects, the impact can be judged in terms of project outcome as well as financial loss. The loss in this case would be the wasted investment as well as the lost opportunity to resolve the pressing business need it was designed to address.

2 Probability. This is normally measured in terms of the likelihood of a risk occurring. In most instances a scale that is non-numeric is chosen, such as high, medium and low or variants on these.

Smart quotes

Formal risk management processes (RMPs) offer a number of important benefits which need to be appreciated if the best use is to be made of RMP. Many people who are not familiar with formal RMPs see them as processes whose whole concern is risk measurement, and see risk measurement as a response to the question 'is this too risky?' in terms of selected performance criteria. Bankers or management boards requiring comfort before releasing funds may seem to be instrumental in causing RMPs to be viewed in this way. There is clearly nothing wrong with banks or boards using risk management to serve this end, but if this is the sole rationale, RMP will be largely wasted, and may prove ineffective in relation to even this limited goal. That is, effective risk measurement may not be feasible unless a richer set of organizational performance criteria is considered.

Chris Chapman and Stephen Ward

When it comes to scoring impact and probability, it is important not to fall into the trap of using the numbers as a surrogate for precision. It is very easy to be seduced into long and tortuous discussions about what the numbers actually mean. By all means, select a simple scale, but do not feel that you need to make it precise. The purpose of the scoring mechanism is to inform judgement, not give an absolute indication of the probability or financial impact. I tend to favour definitions that guide judgement, such as the set below (see Table 4.1). The impact definitions can be altered to meet the specific category of risk or the size of the organization.

As mentioned earlier, the definitions will vary according to the type of risk being assessed. For example:

- In the case of project risk, the impact would be described in terms of project delay, cost overruns and reductions in benefits.

Table 4.1 Quantifying impact and probability

	Impact		Probability
1	Limited or negligible impact on the bottom line – in the region of a few thousand dollars	1	Less than a 25 per cent chance of the risk materializing
2	Minor impact on the bottom line – in the region of a few tens of thousands of dollars	2	Greater than a 25 per cent and less than a 50 per cent chance of the risk materializing
3	Major impact on the bottom line – in the region of many tens of thousands of dollars, and maybe more than one hundred thousand dollars	3	Greater than a 50 per cent and less than a 75 per cent chance of the risk materializing
4	Very significant impact on the bottom line – in the region of hundreds of thousands or perhaps millions of dollars	4	Greater than a 75 per cent chance of the risk materializing

- In the case of environmental risk, the impact would be described in terms of the effect on the local, and perhaps regional, environments (such as rivers, local ecosystems and indigenous wildlife) and also in terms of the subsequent impact on reputation.

- In the case of operational risks, the impact would be described in terms of the disruption caused on the day-to-day business activities.

Once the impact and probability ratings have been agreed for a particular risk, the two are multiplied together to give an indication of how critical the risk might be and hence whether it ought to be managed more actively. Alternatively you can use a graphical device, such as the one in Fig. 4.2 to determine whether a risk is significant or not. The purpose behind this is to ensure management attention is focused on those risks that are the most critical. Without this, good old human nature clicks in once again as we focus on the low risks because they are easy to manage and put off the difficult ones. The stratification also

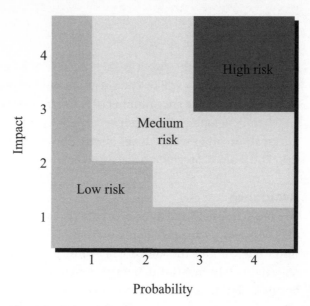

Fig. 4.2   Risk prioritization

Smart answers to tough questions

Q. How do I know when I have the appropriate balance between the need for a formal process that deals with individual risks and integrating risk management within all of the organization's activities?

A. The answer lies in asking your staff if they know what risks are facing their part of the organization and are they managing them effectively. If they can articulate both the risks and the actions being taken to mitigate them then you have the right balance. If they look blank, you know you have a problem; if they can tell you what the risks are but can't describe how they are being addressed then there is an imbalance in favour of integration; if they can describe in detail the process for managing risk but can't highlight the risks facing their part of the enterprise, process has overridden integration.

helps to avoid the problem of having too many risks to manage, something I often encounter when I consult with organizations.

Respond

Having quantified the risk it is then necessary to arrive at an agreed response. Responses will be contingent upon the specific nature of the risk. However, there are a number of basic strategies that can be adopted when developing the response, especially if the risk is considered too great – in other words, it lies outside the organization's appetite for risk. The main strategies are discussed below.

Avoidance

You may choose to avoid the risk entirely by taking a different course of action. In this instance you would still be able to achieve the same result but without the added risk. Thus, in the same way a military objective can be met through more than one course of action, so can a business objective. All that is required is some creative thinking.

Transfer

You may choose to transfer the risk to someone else who might be more expert in its management. In those instances where you do not have the capabilities or expertise to achieve a particular business outcome, you could employ experts who can. For example, many organizations employ consultants or turn to outsourcing to remove the risks associated with delivering a technical project, or managing their IT. Be warned though: just because you have transferred the risk, it does not always mean that you will be free of the consequences of failure. This is particularly true of projects (see 'Smart voices', below).

Smart voices: The Pathway Project[2]

In May 1996 the Benefits Agency of the UK's Department of Social Security and Post Office Counters awarded a contract to ICL computer services group to develop an electronic payment mechanism for paying social security benefits. The electronic system was due to replace the existing paper-based method with a magnetic stripe payment card and to automate payment through the existing network of post offices across the UK. The costs of this project were expected to be in the region of £1 billion and it would take ten months to deliver a live system covering 24 different benefits though 19,000 post offices. This was the first project to be awarded under the UK government's Private Finance Initiative, which was designed to transfer the risks of developing and delivering a working system to the private sector.

By October 1996 a limited system had been implemented in 10 post offices and the project continued to successfully deliver the system with increasing functionality to a further 205 post offices. However, designing and developing a fully functional system proved much more complex and, as a consequence, it took a lot longer than anticipated. Despite replanning the project and deferring the delivery date, the project's time scales and costs continued to escalate and the project was finally cancelled in May 1999. The National Audit Office's review of the project highlighted the following in relation to risk management:

- The project was high risk. It was feasible, but probably not fully deliverable within the very tight timetable originally specified.
- The Department of Social Security's initial business case did not adequately assess the risk and costs of serious slippage.
- The Department of Social Security and Post Office Counters identified most of the risks of the project, but were less successful in assessing their probability and impact.
- A decisive factor in selecting ICL was its acceptance of greater risk.
- The Department of Social Security and Post Office Counters found monitoring and controlling risks very difficult.
- Continuation of the entire project, though apparently the cheapest option, carried significant risks.

The costs of the failure to all parties were significant. The UK government (and hence taxpayer) was left with a bill in excess of £620 million; ICL had to write off £180 million; Post Office Counters wrote off £571 million.

Insuring

The option to insure against a risk means that if financial loss is incurred as a result of the risk maturing then it will be covered by a third-party insurer. Deciding to insure rather than manage the risk has some advantages, not least the ability to almost forget about it. As we saw in Chapter 1, Lloyd's of London was established as a means of insuring against the loss of ships on the high seas. So, if a ship and its cargo were lost, it would not result in the demise of the shipping company.

> **Smart quotes**
>
> Corporations are even more conservative than people. They don't want any downside risk if they can help it – fire, flood, employee injury, quality control mistakes, executives being kidnapped, a mistake by the board of directors. You name the catastrophe, they buy insurance to protect against it.
>
> Sam Hill

However, before adopting the insurance option it is important to weigh up the costs of the insurance premium against the financial implications of the risk. If the premium is greater than the loss associated with the risk, you might be better off accepting the consequences of the risk should it occur and make provisions for it in your budget. Following the terrorist attacks on the World Trade Center in 2001, insurance costs have rocketed, which is making the decision to insure much more complicated. For example, the John Lewis Partnership is reviewing its position after spiralling insurance costs reduced its half-year profits; its insurance costs had doubled to £12 million.[3]

Hedging

Hedging is a process used within most large corporates and financial markets. It is based on the simple precept of offsetting one risk against another, leaving you with no risk. Hedging is therefore a zero-sum game. Many corporations use complex financial instruments, such as forwards, options and swaps, as part of their hedging strategy (see Glossary for descriptions). Companies use these hedging methods to manage the risks associated with their operational activities, including variations in the cost of raw materials, or when developing effective pricing policies for exported goods, as well as balance sheet components such as interest rates. Although popular, a number of commentators believe that hedging distracts management from their core business and because it is a zero-sum game it cannot increase earnings or cashflows and hence cannot increase the value of the enterprise in any lasting way.

Diversification

This is the classic avoidance of having all your eggs in one basket, and it is practised by venture capitalists very successfully. Diversification recognizes that not every investment, or business objective, will be achieved and the best way to hedge against failure is to spread your bets.

Having determined the response to the risk, it is important to ensure that it is owned by a specific individual who will be charged with its management. As we saw with the Pathway Project, organizations can struggle with the management of risks and especially those that are complex or beyond their technical capability. Therefore, choosing who should manage the risk is something that should not be done lightly, as allocating it to someone who is not able, or perhaps is unwilling, to manage the risk is often fatal. Who should be responsible will depend on the type of risk being managed. If it is strategic, it ought to be owned by someone with the authority to take strategic decisions, such as the board. Similarly, if it is a project risk, it should fall within the remit of the project manager.

Manage

The final stage in the risk management process involves managing and monitoring the risks. This requires the organization to manage those risks that matter by following through on the agreed actions associated with the chosen response and monitoring the risks in relation to the wider organizational and external environments. When it comes to managing risk, I believe it is far better to focus effort on managing the top ten risks than attempting to manage hundreds. Naturally, you cannot dismiss or ignore those risks that are rated lower as, like everything else in organizational life, these may change. Therefore, as a rule of thumb:

- Always actively manage those risks that have been rated as high.

- Keep an active watch on those risks that have been rated as medium by reviewing them regularly.

- Keep an occasional watch on the minor risks, but do not spend too much time on these to the detriment of the medium and high risks. In some cases you can afford to ignore them, as the effort and perhaps cost of managing them may outweigh the impact should they mature. Once again, it is necessary to apply judgement.

Smart quotes

Enronitis provoked one of the most serious bouts of soul-searching in American history. For a huge variety of commentators this was clear evidence of a crisis: a crisis in morality and ethics; a crisis of corporate governance; a crisis in corporate America. As the television beamed pictures of sad-looking executives being handcuffed and taken away by the authorities, magazine columnists asked: Is capitalism sick? Elsewhere, one television journalist perhaps summed up the mood by stating, in official tones, that 'lying, stealing and cheating are at the heart of the US financial system'.

Peter Bernstein

One of the best ways to manage risks is to establish an appropriate risk governance framework, as described in the next section. This should be supported by a clear articulation of the risks and a suitable set of documentation. I favour a simple risk register, such as the one illustrated below in Table 4.2. By keeping it simple and focused, the organization can concentrate its risk management activities more effectively and avoid the obvious problems associated with long and convoluted processes.

The final aspect to the manage stage is to recognize that sometimes you will fail to manage the occasional risk adequately and hence may have to invoke prepared contingency plans. Such contingency planning lies at the heart of business continuity planning and crisis management. As expected, many organizations have pre-prepared responses to events such as loss of technology systems, industrial disputes, product failures, fire and so on. The nature of these plans falls out of the risk management process and, in the case of business continuity planning, often involves annual rehearsals. For example, some companies simulate a major disaster to test how quickly business-as-usual activities can be restored. This helps to keep the plan current and the staff familiar with how to respond. In addition, where the media is involved, staff

Smart voices: Responding to competitive pressures[4]

Three hardware shop owners shared the same frontage, with each shop adjacent to the next. Sales were flat and the owner of the end of the frontage decided to improve sales by putting the following sign up: 'Year end clearance'. In response, the owner of the shop at the other end of the frontage put up the following sign: 'Annual close out'. Clearly, the owner of the middle shop was at risk of losing significant amounts of business if he did not respond. After some careful thinking, he added the sign 'Main entrance'. So, although he was unable to control his competitors, he was smart in how he responded to the risk that he was exposed to.

Table 4.2 A simple risk register

Description	Scenario for maturity	Impact	Probability	Priority score	Management strategy	Containment strategy
This should provide a clear description of the risk. In general, a single line description is inadequate. The purpose here is to describe it so that everyone who needs to be aware of the risk understands it, not just the person managing it	This describes how the risk will materialize. To do this it is necessary to describe the most likely series of events that will lead to the risk maturing. The purpose of this is to sensitize the organization and those who will be expected to manage the risk to the leading indicators that the risk will mature	The impact, from 1 to 4, based on agreed definitions	The probability, from 1 to 4, based upon agreed definitions	The combined score of multiplying the Impact score with the probability score. This will be used to focus management action on those risks that are of the highest priority (usually with a score of 12 and above)	This details the actions that will be undertaken to manage the risk. This will include the agreed response and the individual responsible for the risk. Note that other people may be involved in the execution of the actions, but the owner will be ultimately accountable	This describes the actions that will be taken to address the risk once it materializes. In other words, where the management actions have failed to contain the risk. Where this occurs the organization will need to respond immediately, which may involve them invoking crisis management procedures

are trained in how to deal with the press, television and radio during a crisis (see 'Smart people to have on your side: John Clare', below).

Smart people to have on your side: John Clare

John Clare is a former ITN and *Daily Mail* journalist and author of *John Clare's Guide to Media Handling*. As one of the UK's leading media and crisis consultants, Clare believes that there is a clear connection between the media headline and the company's bottom line, and he provides sound advice on how to deal with the media during a crisis.

The four pillars of risk management

As a basic process, the above works well in most situations. However, organizations often have to tailor their risk processes to meet the specific needs of the different types of risks they have to manage, which in some cases requires a more sophisticated approach. For example, managing financial risks in a publicly quoted company requires more complex approaches to meet regulatory needs, such as Basal, as well as to provide comfort to the company's shareholders.

Could you handle a crisis?

Irrespective of tailoring, any effective risk management process requires the four pillars of risk management to be in place (see Fig. 4.1, p. 125). Once established, the interaction between the process and these four underlying components should lead to a system that is capable of serving the organization in every type of risk it faces. The following paragraphs briefly outline the four pillars (which are discussed in greater detail in other chapters).

Define risk framework

The Network for Environmental Risk Assessment and Management define a risk framework as:

*a description of an organizational specific set of functional activities and associ-
ated definitions that define the risk management system in an organization and
the relationship to the risk management organizational system. A risk management framework defines the processes and the order and timing of the processes
that will be used to manage risks.*

A risk management framework thus underpins both the types of risks
that the organization is likely to face and how the process needs to be
tailored to the various categories of risk it needs to address. A useful
starting point for developing such a framework would be Chapter 2,
which deals with the major categories of risk that a typical corporate
is likely to face. Having selected those that are relevant, the next step
would be to understand how these relate to the strategic objectives of
the firm, the associated critical success factors and the major functions
and activities, such as projects and programmes, operations and so on.
The framework must therefore define the what and the why of risk
management. The how is addressed by the process. Finally, it should
identify where in the organization the risks are likely to lie and who
will be responsible for their management.

Articulate risk appetite

As we discussed in the previous chapter, determining your risk appetite is critical. Knowing which risks you are willing to take, and those
that you are not, allows the organization to influence its future. So, as
well as avoiding those risks it feels would be too great to take, it also
helps to focus on those risks that it is willing to run with. Establishing
the boundary between acceptable and unacceptable risks is therefore
what risk appetite is all about. However, in order to create the basis
of an enterprise-wide risk management approach, it is necessary to
articulate it on a much wider footing. Thus, articulating your risk appetite in the context of formalizing the process is essential for the following reasons:

- It helps in the prioritizing of risks and, through this, it ensures that the organization focuses on those risks that matter and which can yield the highest return.

- It allows everyone across the enterprise to understand the risks that the organization is prepared to take and hence helps to frame their own risk management activities.

- It sensitizes everyone to those risks that are considered unacceptable.

Create risk culture

Many organizations talk about developing a risk culture in which everyone, irrespective of what position they hold, is able to take risks that progress the company or which can help their particular function meet the strategic objectives of the business. Unfortunately, many organizations pay lip service to this and end up with a risk-averse culture or one that is too unforgiving to encourage risk taking. All too often there is too much ground between rhetoric and reality. You know when an organization has no risk culture when:

Do you use the risk management process to cover your tracks or deflect blame, or as a genuine way to encourage the taking of appropriate risk?

- Someone takes a risk and they are sacked.

- Someone would like to take a risk, but the answer is always no.

- The status quo rules and no one wants to rock the boat.

Without a healthy risk culture most risk management processes will fail because they will be perceived as nothing more than a tool for covering your arse! Because this is such an important topic, I have dedicated the next chapter to it.

Establish risk governance

The governance of risk has long been a concern to regulators who are there to protect the investor from the worst excesses of executive and corporate behaviour. In most respects, the driver of corporate regulation – and especially that associated with risk management – has been the major corporate scandals, blackholes and bubbles identified in the introduction. The key standards for the control of risks that have been introduced are as follows:

- The Committee of Sponsoring Organizations for the Treadway Commission (COSO) (US), which addresses the internal control systems within organizations (covering the control environment, risk assessment, control activities, information and communication, and monitoring).

- The Cadbury and the Combined Code (UK), which is similar to COSO and requires all publicly quoted companies to review their internal controls.

- The Turnbull Report, which argued that boards of listed companies should report annually on their risk assessment and decision-making processes.

- The Criteria of Control Board (CoCo) (Canada), which extends COSO to define 20 criteria for effective control under four groupings: purpose; commitment; capability; monitoring and learning.

- The Control objectives for information and related Technologies (CobiT), which sets a general foundation for security and control in IT at an international level. The model identifies control objectives under five IT domains: planning, organization, delivery, support and monitoring.

- Bank for International Settlements (BIS), which has produced a framework for internal controls in banking organizations.

- The Sarbanes-Oxley Act (US), which requires US chief executives to certify their financial statements, disclose material from off-balance-sheet transactions and confirm that their control environment is fully documented and working.

Naturally, organizations should not rely on regulators to define their governance requirements for them; instead they should ensure that responsibilities for risk management are clearly defined throughout the entire enterprise. With an increasing focus on shareholder value and value-based reporting, the responsibilities for risk reporting have grown considerably. As a result, organizations have established various committees that focus on their major areas of risk. For example:

- Business and strategic risk committees, which involve the senior executives of the organization, including the non-executive directors. Such committees address the external risks the company is facing and the most significant internal risks. This committee is often chaired by the CEO.

- Project and programme boards, which focus on the management of the major risks that affect the successful delivery of the business's

Smart people to have on your side: The Office of Government Commerce

The OGC develops best-practice guidelines for the UK government. It has defined the following nine-step risk management process:

1 define a framework
2 identify the risks
3 identify probable risk owners
4 evaluate the risks
5 set acceptable levels of risk
6 identify suitable responses to risk
7 implement responses
8 gain assurances about effectiveness
9 embed and review.

In addition, the OGC has identified the following critical success factors for risk management:

- Clearly identified senior management to support, own and lead on risk management.
- Risk management policies and the benefits of effective management clearly communicated to all staff.
- Existence and adoption of a framework for all management of risk that is transparent and repeatable.
- Existence of an organizational culture that supports well thought-through risk taking and innovation.
- Management of risk fully embedded in management processes and consistently applied.
- Management of risk closely linked to achievement of objectives.
- Risks associated with working with other organizations explicitly assessed and managed.
- Risks actively monitored and regularly reviewed on a constructive 'no-blame' basis.

major change initiatives. This committee involves the members of the project/programme team and key stakeholders and is chaired by the sponsor.

- Operational risk management committees, which focus on the wide-ranging risks that affect the operational viability of the organization. The membership of this committee will vary according to the nature of the operational risk being faced, but will probably involve internal audit and be chaired by a senior operational executive such as the COO.

- Financial risk committees, which focus on the major financial risks arising from the treasury function, credit risks and other financial risks not addressed elsewhere. This committee is usually chaired by the CFO.

In addition to the various risk committees, there are key risk management roles that should be assigned to specific individuals and functions within the organization. Table 4.3 shows advice offered by The Institute of Internal Auditors Research Foundation[5] regarding where responsibility for risk management lies (with some additions).

In this chapter we have reviewed in some detail the basic risk management process. Process is clearly important but, in order to be truly effective, it has to be appropriate for both the organization and the types of risks being managed. Achieving this means:

- defining a risk management framework that places risk management in the organizational context;

- ensuring the organization's risk appetite is articulated to everyone within the company so that they are clear on what risks they can and cannot take;

- establishing a genuine risk culture so that people will not be persecuted for taking risks and failing; and

- introducing and bedding-in risk governance mechanisms.

Table 4.3 Risk management roles and responsibilities

Chief executive	Drives the focus on risk management throughout the whole organization
	Is ultimately responsible and accountable for all risks that affect the viability and profitability of the organization
	Must understand the extent of the organization's most significant risks and ensure they are managed
	Is responsible for developing a healthy balance between risk and reward
	Must ensure that an appropriate risk culture is established and maintained across the enterprise
Chief financial officer	Responsible for all financial risk management activities
	Acts on behalf of the chief executive in implementing a suitable risk management architecture
	Responsible for maintaining an effective balance between risk and opportunity
	Works closely with the treasury function (if one exists) to understand the organization's approach to minimizing its exposure to financial risk
Chief risk officer	Works with the organization to implement a risk architecture through which all risks will be managed
	Ensures the risk architecture is suitably maintained and updated when required
	Monitors risk on an ongoing basis and manages and reports on the organization's risk profile
	Works closely with the owners of the major risks to ensure they appropriately management
	Helps to identify all major risks and resolution strategies
Internal audit	Operationally responsible for the continuous assessment of risk within the organization
	This is usually conducted through a series of rolling audits to ensure all operating units are managing risk appropriately
	Provides advice and guidance on matters of risk across all operating divisions
	Reports directly into the audit committee, and often the board
Project and programme managers	Specifically responsible for the active management of those risks that can affect the outcome of the project or programme
	Ensures that any project or programme risks that could have a significant business impact are raised with either the chief risk officer or chief financial officer
Business unit managers/ directors	Responsible for the management of operational and functional risks within their business unit
	Ensures any risks that have wider business impacts are raised with the chief risk officer or chief financial officer

With all this in place, the organization will be in a strong position to address the risks it faces successfully.

The next chapter reviews what we know about organizational culture and how this impacts the creation of an open and honest risk culture. After all, if companies are genuinely interested in creating a risk culture, they would be wise to understand a little bit about organizational culture before they try to establish one that is focused on risk. For some this might prove to be very difficult indeed.

Notes

1   OECD (2001) *The Hidden Threat to e-Government: Avoiding Large Government IT Failures*, p. 3.

2   NAO (2000) *The Cancellation of The Benefits Payment Card Project*, London: The Stationery Office.

3   Voyle, S. (2002) 'Insurance costs dent John Lewis', *Financial Times*, p. 24.

4   This story is taken from Miner, I. (1999) *The World's Best Marketing Secret*, Oxford: Capstone Publishing, pp. 30–31.

5   Steinberg, R. and Bromilow, C. (2000) *Corporate Governance and the Board: What Works Best*, Florida: The Institute of Internal Auditors Research Foundation, p. 17.

5 Smart Thinking III: Develop a Risk Culture

Smart quotes

Culture has become a powerful way to hold a company together against a tidal wave of pressures for disintegration, such as decentralisation, downsizing, and de-layering. At the same time the traditional mechanisms for integration – hierarchies and control systems, among other devices – are proving costly and ineffective. Culture is what remains to bolster a company's identity and without it a company lacks value, direction and purpose.

Rob Goffee and Gareth Jones

Culture. Many organizations talk about it. Few understand it. Most play lip service to it. This is especially true when it comes to developing a risk culture. The difficulty of developing such a culture should never be underestimated. It is not easy for any organization to develop a truly risk-embracing culture and those that purport to have one are not always being honest with themselves, their staff or their external stakeholders.

The first sign that a risk culture has failed is when someone is sacked, castigated or generally hauled over the coals when they take a risk and fail. Whistle-blowing is also a good indicator. When someone believes that the company is doing something illegal and decides to make their feelings known to a government or law enforcement agency they are often discredited and sacked. In such situations it is clear that the organization is not one that embraces risk or an open policy of raising concerns. Fortunately, and as long as the company has broken the law, the whistle-blower is protected and can sue if they are harassed of sacked.

The consequences for anyone who is prepared to go public on an issue can be catastrophic, as we saw with the apparent suicide of the Ministry of Defence official, Dr David Kelly, whose hounding by a number of politicians led him to take his own life. The politicians concerned bullied Dr Kelly in order to save face following the 'sexing-up' of the dossier that led to the Second Gulf War and the toppling of the Iraqi regime. Following the Hutton enquiry, which was designed to establish the truth about the whole affair, Alastair Campbell, Tony Blair's closet aide and director of communication, dramatically resigned. If nothing else this clearly demonstrates that there is no risk culture in central government. Although extreme, similar situations are played out in many other organizations, which on face value appear to embrace risk, but deep down harbour a strong fear of failure. They would rather make someone a scapegoat than accept they might be wrong. The benefits of establishing a genuine risk culture can be significant, however,

Smart quotes

As Karl Popper pointed out some time ago, the Open Society, that is a world of continuous investigation and assessment of nature and social relations, has many enemies. Most human beings prefer certainty above all else. Most innovations and change threaten such orderliness. In particular, new ideas can be subversive and dangerous. Much of history shows the tendency of thought systems to close down, solidify and put up increasing barriers to any disturbance.

Alan Macfarlane and Gerry Martin

as it is the ability to take risks that is one of the most significant drivers of innovation and, more importantly, profit.

Before we can explore what developing a risk culture means in practice, it is worth spending a little time looking at organizational culture itself.

Understanding culture

Culture is often boiled down to the 'way we do things around here'. And, the 'way we do things around here' is usually considered to encapsulate a number of things including the shared assumptions, behaviours and habits of those employed by the organization, together with the symbols and language used to reinforce the organization's core values. This shared meaning is typically expressed both formally, through the rules, structure, hierarchy, pay and reward mechanisms of the organization, and informally, through the way teams function and the way individuals are treated by their peers. Culture is also believed to be created and reinforced through the primary processes of the organization, including:

- rules and policies

- goals and measures

- rewards and recognition

- staffing and selection

- training and development

- ceremonies and events

- leadership and behaviour

- communications

- the physical environment

- organizational structure.

As the processes connected with these ten areas are brought into contact during each working day, they collectively make up the environment that surrounds the workforce. This organizational environment in turn creates and reinforces the organization's culture. Process is, of course, not the only thing that forms and perpetuates culture, as the desire to conform and be part of a cohesive group is a strong influence on developing habitual behaviours and predictability within individuals. Moreover, predictability is believed to be the mainstay of organizational and individual performance, and it is this that creates the common behaviours that can be called culture.

It follows therefore that those who act in an unpredictable way in relation to the prevailing norms of behaviour will not survive for long. None of us should underestimate how culture affects the way we behave and, when it comes to risk, how we perceive and behave when we are faced with a hazard.

Culture affects us at four different levels, as discussed below.

Smart quotes

Research has shown that many of the organizations that are successful in the constantly changing business environment place a premium on innovation, risk-taking and entrepreneurship and strive to develop a 'breakthrough' culture – a culture where ongoing experimentation thrives.

Chris Frost, David Allen, James Porter, Philip Bloodworth

The national level

The way we are brought up in our home countries impacts us in many different ways. It frames, among other things, how we interact with people we don't know, what our general attitudes are towards work, how we perceive the legal system, how we raise our children and our general views of what is right and wrong. As we all know, national cultures vary considerably and often cause confusion, annoyance and amusement. Indeed, the very fact that we joke about different nationalities demonstrates how different people from other countries behave (see 'Smart people to have on your side: Geert Hofstede', below)

Smart people to have on your side: Geert Hofstede

Hofstede is Professor of Organizational Anthropology and International Management at the University of Limburg in Maastricht, the Netherlands, and founder of the Institute for Research on Intercultural Cooperation. He is the author of numerous books on national cultures and how to manage cross-national teams and he has developed a model of national culture with four dimensions:

1   Power distance. Hofstede defined this as the extent to which the less powerful members of institutions and organizations within a country expect and accept that power is distributed unequally. In practice this means the degree to which subordinates are willing to question their superiors and push back against decisions. Such push-back is more prevalent in Western societies and less common in the Far East. Where the acceptance of inequality is greatest, paternalistic and autocratic management styles tend to dominate (such as in Japan), while the opposite is true in those countries where inequality is less acceptable. Here, management tends to be more consultative. This is typical of the Low Countries.

2   Individualism–collectivism. This refers to the extent to which people within a society are expected to fend for themselves and their immediate families. The more one is expected to fend for oneself,

the more individualistic the society. The opposite of this is collectivism where, from birth, people are integrated into strong, cohesive groups that tend to be maintained throughout life. As is to be expected, in those societies that are more collective, decision making tends to be group-based and, as a consequence, often slower (for example, the Nordic countries) than in those countries that are more individualistic (for example, the US and the UK). This has implications on how the relationship between individuals needs to be formed, because it is this that creates the basis of trust. Because collective societies tend to be dominated by the family unit, those outside are viewed suspiciously until such time they can earn the trust of the family. This explains why in some countries, such as China and southern Italy, there are very few large organizations. The majority tend to be family owned. The same applies to North African countries. The opposite is normally true in individualistic societies, where people are more willing to trust those they come into contact with.

3   Masculinity–femininity. In those societies that can be considered masculine, emphasis tends to be placed on achievement, ambition and success (for example, the US), while in those countries that are more feminine, the emphasis is on quality of work and caring for others (for example, Finland, Holland and Sweden). As expected, in those countries that are more masculine, working hours tend to be longer. In the more feminine cultures, work is a means to an end, not an end in itself.

4   Uncertainty avoidance. This refers to the extent to which members of a culture feel threatened by uncertain or unknown circumstances. In those countries where uncertainty avoidance is high, people attempt to reduce it through structure, process and familiarity, so that events are clearly interpretable. This is true of Germany, Switzerland and France. In addition, where uncertainty avoidance is high, people are less likely to question superiors and tend to avoid situations that involve conflict. In those countries that have a weak uncertainty avoidance, there tends to be less concern or need for strict rules; people are generally more self-governing, conflict is seen as non-threatening and an important part of the workplace and individuals are generally more flexible. This is typical of the US, the UK and Australia.

The organizational level

As we identified above, an organization's norms of behaviour dictate how we behave in the work setting. Every organization has a culture, even if it has not been explicitly defined or enshrined. The company in which you work will have a set of unwritten rules that you must adhere to if you are to be successful. And I am sure that you have seen people advance the career ladder with apparent ease without necessarily adding much intrinsic value. These are the people who have sussed out the company culture. Those who want to get on but are less successful tend to be oblivious to the company culture and will struggle to achieve things that make little difference to their career. An organization's culture will drive how people relate to each other, how things get done and, most importantly, what drives it (see 'Smart people to have on your side: Rob Goffee and Gareth Jones', below).

Smart people to have on your side: Rob Goffee and Gareth Jones

Goffee and Jones are the authors of *The Character of a Corporation*, in which they developed a model of culture based upon two dimensions – sociability and solidarity. Sociability is measure of the friendliness between members of the organization, and is considered to promote teamwork and creativity. It also creates an environment in which people are willing to go that extra mile. Solidarity is based on common tasks, mutual interests, and clearly understood shared goals that benefit all parties, irrespective of whether they like each other. In this case, there is more emphasis on task than relationships. The combination of sociability and solidarity allowed them to derive four cultures:

1   The *networked* culture is typically one that exudes friendship and kindness. People genuinely like each other and display high levels of empathy. There also tends to be a high degree of trust between them. The networked organization is typically conversational, with people entering into discussions that cover all topics, from

work to what they did over the weekend. This emphasis on friendship displays itself in the value placed on patience and tolerance, as people are able to have their say without getting talked down. The office space tends to be personalized and an open-door policy predominates. Time is taken to socialize both within and outside work. The communication process tends to be both formalized, through face-to-face discussions and in meetings, and informal, as part of the general socializing outside the workplace. Examples of organizations with networked cultures include Unilever, Heineken and Philips.

2   The *mercenary* culture is restless and ruthless, with a powerful drive to get things done. Goals tend to be at the forefront of people's minds, as they strive to make things happen. Time between coming up with an idea and executing it is short; time is everything, as is action. Winning is very important to the mercenary organization and those within it. Mercenary organizations achieve their external goals by setting very high internal ones, using targets and objectives to get there. Communication is swift and to the point. Getting the job done may entail long hours, as leaving before the job is finished is usually frowned upon. Value is placed on reacting quickly and not overdoing the thinking time. Examples include Citicorp, PepsiCo and Mars.

3   The *communal* culture is one that combines the friendship associated with the networked culture and the drive and ambition of the mercenary culture. Passion for the company and its products go hand in hand with a strong sense of community and shared responsibility. Organizations that fall into the communal culture tend to have a work-hard, play-hard ethos about them that is highly infectious. Office space tends to be shared, and there are few barriers between functions. Communication is everywhere, with every channel being used (meetings, face-to-face, corridors and so on). Work and non-work life meld into one, with work becoming a way of life. More importantly, people live and breathe the organization and its mission; they are almost evangelical about it. Examples include Hewlett-Packard and Johnson & Johnson.

4   Within the *fragmented* culture people are not particularly friendly toward each other, and they do not support the organization or its goals; they work at an organization, but primarily for themselves. People tend to favour working in isolation and uninterrupted. As

a result, doors tend to be closed, and offices are well equipped for self-contained work. Work is often conducted at home, or on the road, and not always in the office; being away from the office is usually a sign that they are busy (such as with clients). People tend to associate more with their profession than the organization. Communication is usually work related, and brief. And, because people are often absent, few meetings take place. A good example of the fragmented culture is Chrysler, which in the late 1970s exhibited many of the dysfunctional qualities of the fragmented culture. Government and academic institutions are also strongly fragmented, which helps to explain why Tony Blair's drive to joined-up government in the UK is destined to failure.

The real power of the Goffee and Jones model lies in its ability to describe four basic organizational cultures without needing to go into esoteric descriptions. Moreover, because it describes the cultures so well, it is easy to pin individual observations against it, including those associated with risk.

The functional level

While it is often convenient to refer to the organization as if it had a single homogeneous culture, this is rarely the case, because this single culture will encapsulate a number of subcultures. Such heterogeneity results from the differentiation that exists within organizations as they establish different functions to perform a specific type of work.

It should be clear that cultural variations exist between finance, marketing, IT and other organizational divisions. Such differences exist because of the physical separation of the functions, the training they receive, the types of work they perform and the conditions they work under. For example, the finance department has a fundamentally different culture to the marketing department because it focuses on the financial health of the organization, while marketing focuses on the development and marketing of the organization's products, as well as establishing and promoting its brands. The skills, practices and policies valued in one area will not necessarily be valued in another. The challenge for most organizations is therefore to ensure that their organizational culture is strong enough to allow functions to cooperate over corporate issues. This is particularly the case with risk management.

The team level

Those who have worked within high-performing teams know how unbeatable they can be. The converse is true, as working in a dysfunctional team can be a miserable experience. Teams form their own micro culture created by the team's leader, the people who sit within it and the nature of their activities. Like culture in general, it gives everyone a sense of identity and sets them aside from everyone else. Most teams form around projects, which, as we saw within Chapter 2, are one major source of risk. Clearly, if a team is performing poorly, the risks of failure can be very significant. But even when a team is performing very well there are still risks associated with overcommitment.

Culture and its relationship with risk

Smart quotes:

I came to see, in my time at IBM, that culture isn't just one aspect of the game – it is the game. In the end, an organization is nothing more than the collective capacity of its people to create value.

Louis V. Gerstner Jr

Those who have to work across cultures, be they international or within a single company, should be wary of the pitfalls of stereotyping others and assuming that other people think the same. But how does culture play into risk and risk management?

If we revisit the works of both Hofstede, and Jones and Goffee, we can see some interesting dynamics that have a bearing on how organizations deal with risk. Taking nationality first: looking at Hofstede's dimension of uncertainty avoidance seems to hold the key to whether or not someone is generally risk averse or risk seeking. Those who hail from countries with a high uncertainty avoidance tend to view conflict as threatening, need to avoid failure, need to have consensus (in other words, they do not like to go out on a limb), tend to feel more anxious, prefer to have laws and rules that govern behaviour and activities, and become more stressful in uncertain conditions. Countries that fall into this category include Germany, Switzerland, Austria and Japan.

Now compare people from these countries to those that hail from the US, the UK, Hong Kong, Singapore and India, which have low uncertainty avoidance. People from these countries are typically less stressed, view conflict and competition as fair play, like flexibility, accept dissent and do not need strict rules and regulations to operate in. It should come as no surprise, then, that the US is the main driver of the market economy in which risk taking and uncertainty are key. Here, fluidity in the employment market and less regulation provide the foundation for innovation and experimentation. Similarly, India is increasingly playing an important role in the global economy as it focuses on high-tech back-office and IT outsourcing. The converse is true across most of Europe, which is suffering from too much rigidity in the employment market, too much social engineering and a preponderance for inaction rather than innovation. National culture, it seems, is a major factor in how competitive, innovative and risk taking a nation is.

Looking at the organizational level also suggests that some cultures are more comfortable with taking risk than others. For example, the Goffee and Jones model of organizational culture suggests that:

Smart voices: Marsh[1]

Marsh, the world's biggest insurance broker of mid-size organizations recently conducted a survey into risk attitude across Europe and found the following differences:

- UK, German and Italian companies recognized the need to understand risk and to treat it as a priority.
- German organizations were more likely to believe that business was risky and claimed to know better the risks they faced than anyone else.
- Belgian and French companies claimed to know their customers and suppliers so well that their business risks were low.
- UK companies believed that there was a direct correlation between risk management and shareholder value. Italian businesses held the opposite view.
- The majority of European businesses believed that strategic and operational risk were the most significant, while in the UK, the major risks were associated with loss of key staff, absenteeism and breakdowns in the supply chain.
- Italian and Spanish companies were particularly concerned with external risks, such as increased competition.

- Networked cultures will take calculated risks only and do not generally like to take risks that could bet the company. When they take risks, a lot of time is spent analysing the implications and assessing alternative options. This slows the process down (which suits the culture). The only exception is when there is a sudden change in fortunes, which is usually the result of an externally imposed risk or event, such as a hostile takeover.

- Fragmented cultures do not like risk at all. In fact they prefer to avoid it as much as possible because they do not want to lose face. Just think of government and how it approaches risk, especially those associated with major change projects. Because many of these fail, those in charge are expert at deflecting the blame onto other factors, people or events. Rarely do they admit that they have screwed up. At the individual level, however, people can take risks that are not visible to the business as a whole. This can present real and significant dangers to the organization if these are left unchecked (which they so often are).

- Mercenary cultures embrace risk but will always sack those that take risks and fail. Fear of failure looms very large in these organizations and, although generally market driven and reactive, no one likes to take a risk that could expose them. As a result, people will hide any issues and concerns they have and, if they are personally exposed, they will attempt to deal with it themselves rather than raise it to a higher authority. This is classic behaviour in the financial markets, where the likes of Nick Leeson feel compelled to hide their losses instead of coming clean. This only compounds the problem and increases the risk.

- Communal cultures embrace risk for all the right reasons and are willing to learn from mistakes. This is an organization that sees risk and risk taking as an integral part of its ethos. In fact, not taking risk is perceived to be more of a problem than taking it. Naturally, taking risk is one thing, but taking those over which you have no control is another. When we look back on the worst excesses of the dotcom boom and bust, many start-ups took outlandish risks and failed to manage them. It's no wonder that most failed.

There is another dynamic, which may also have a bearing on whether an organization is prepared to take risks, and this also plays into the generation of a risk culture. This is to do with the response to failure and, given that taking risks can result in failure, this is a significant concern when attempting to make a risk culture stick. It is common for organizations to react in a number of ways when faced with a failure. The form the response takes depends on the degree to which a fear of

Smart quotes

Only in cultures that have transformational leadership, in which leaders lead as well as manage, do you get an environment where mistakes are tolerated. Those cultures are aware that you can gain from mistakes, which may often be the result of trying to do something in a more innovative or creative way. If you create a blame culture, people will not want to take creative risks.

Professor Cary Cooper

failure exists within the organization and whether or not executives are willing to forgive staff when errors are made (see Fig. 5.1).

There are four basic ways in which an organization can respond to failure.

1 Where the fear of failure is high and the culture unforgiving there is a tendency to blame and sack staff rather than learn from the failure. In such instances, the blame and associated removal of staff is normally misdirected and is rarely the result of a full and

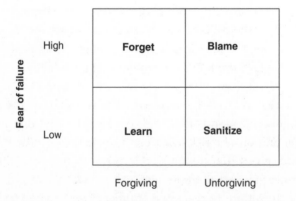

Fig. 5.1 Failure, fear and response

thorough analysis of both what went wrong and where the true accountability lay. The problem with this type of reaction is that it creates a culture in which the fear of failure is reinforced. It also tends to increase the likelihood of the irrational behaviours. People also fear that they can become tarnished by association when an initiative fails or a risk blows up. As a result, and as a means of protecting themselves, the behaviours will shift towards the non-disclosure of problems, and this creates an environment in which the early resolution of risks and issues becomes almost impossible.

2   In organizations where the fear of failure is equally high, but the culture more forgiving, there is a bias toward brushing the failure under the carpet and trying to forget that it ever happened. In both cases the opportunity for learning is typically lost and the organization is destined to repeat the same errors of judgement in future projects.

3   Where the fear of failure is low and culture unforgiving, the usual response to failure is a 'going through the motions' post-failure analysis in which the reasons for the failure are analysed, reviewed, sanitized and stored without ever reaching those people that could truly benefit. It is as though there is a need to wring the organization's hands as a means of exorcizing the failure. Learning is therefore restricted to a limited number of people, and the experience adds no intrinsic value to the future management of risk.

4   Where the culture is more forgiving and the fear of failure low, the organization is able to genuinely learn from the experience of failure and feed this into the management of future risks. Needless to say, such organizations appear to be very rare.

Creating a risk culture

Smart quotes

Risk culture is the degree to which management recognizes the need for risk management competency within the organization. It encompasses an organisation's appetite and tolerance for risk in its daily operating activities and decision-making processes. An organization with a strong risk culture is committed to the establishment of standards and protocols for identifying, assessing and managing risks.

PricewaterhouseCoopers

Any chief executive would agree that creating a culture that accepts and embraces risk is essential to driving future profitability. After all, there is plenty of anecdotal evidence to suggest this is true. Furthermore, they would also agree that the increasing complexity of the business environment necessitates a more mature approach to managing risk. Organizations can no longer afford to maintain a culture that blames, ignores or sanitizes failure, as this prevents risks from being spotted in the first place, let alone managed and reported on. Creating a no-surprise culture means allowing everyone to raise concerns and issues as they go about their daily work. Sanctioning those that highlight risks or those that fail only helps to push risk management off the agenda and promote a culture of self-preservation. In the long run this stifles innovation and results in a culture where no one is willing to take risks. But how can enterprises create a risk culture?

According to PricewaterhouseCoopers, there are four key attributes that define a strong risk culture:

1   Leadership and strategy. This dimension demonstrates ethics and values throughout the organization as well the way in which it communicates its missions and objectives.

Smart people to have on your side: Michael Pearn, Chris Mulrooney and Tim Payne

Pearn, Mulrooney and Payne are consultants with occupational psychologists Pearn Kandola and authors of *Ending the Blame Culture*. They believe that making mistakes is a powerful way to learn important lessons, both in life and in the workplace. They state that blame cultures are based on the negative power of mistakes. This is because making mistakes is unpleasant and threatens our self-esteem. We fear the consequences of making mistakes, especially if these are punished. They have developed the INVEST framework, which allows organizations to enhance learning though the better management of mistakes:

- **I**nspired learners – are employees motivated, willing and able to learn? Do they take calculated risks?
- **N**urturing environment – does it support and allow experiment and challenge?
- **V**ision for the future – is there one that people aspire to? Does the organization see itself as continuously learning in an unpredictable world?
- **E**nhancement of learning – does the organization systematically use techniques to enhance the learning potential and capabilities of everyone?
- **S**upportive managers – do they tolerate and learn from mistakes?
- **T**ransforming structures – is cross-functional working encouraged? Do existing structures enable or even foster mistakes?

2   Accountability and reinforcement. This reveals the organization's ability to assign individual accountability while measuring and rewarding performance.

3   People and communications. This indicates how an organization shares knowledge and information and develops competence within its employees.

4   Risk management and infrastructure. This identifies how good the organization is at assessing and measuring risk and its ability to

Do you trust your staff enough to allow them to take risks, and do they believe you?

take the necessary steps to establish effective processes and controls.

The ideal profile, which would indicate a concrete risk management culture, would be one in which:

- Leadership and strategy are strong, starting at the top and evident at all leadership and management levels throughout the organization.

- Accountability and reinforcement is clearly defined and understood throughout the hierarchy. In other words, everyone understands their role in the management of risk, as well as the boundaries in which they are permitted to operate.

- People and communications support the identification, communication and management of risks, again at all levels.

- Risk management and infrastructure are designed to facilitate the capture and management of risk. Processes are appropriate and tailored to each risk category and suitable technologies are available to model the consequences of risk, aid decision making about the acceptance and options associated with individual risks, and maintain and monitor a collective understanding of all the major risks that the enterprise is exposed to.

An effective risk management culture also depends on the following:

Leadership

A risk management culture must, of course, begin with the board of directors, because if it fails here, it will fail throughout the entire organization. The appointment of a chief risk officer at board level is a positive action that clearly demonstrates the commitment to the management

Smart answers to tough questions[2]

Q. How do you know when you have created an effective risk culture?

A. You will know when people at all levels within the organization think and behave in the following way:

1   There are no excuses. Everyone takes active responsibility for managing risks. No one has to make apologies for identifying risks.
2   There is no complaining. Each person accepts that things can go wrong, that mistakes are made and that, sometimes, positive outcomes appear elusive.
3   There are no cover-ups. Everyone is truthful, open and candid. Any issues, concerns and problems are communicated promptly and asking for help is not a sign of weakness.
4   There are no blind spots. Everyone understands that taking risk is closely associated with opportunity. And, although they are aware of the potential downside, they seek out the upside.

of risk. Similar roles need to be established across each of the major functions to ensure full coverage, commitment and, most importantly, that leadership is present across the entire enterprise.

Commitment

Leadership without commitment will not create or preserve a risk culture. To that end the board must allocate risk management responsibilities among its senior executives and these senior managers must be made to realize that their jobs are in jeopardy if there are major failures in control that could have been prevented through effective risk management. In the same vein, the board must not merely pay lip service to the need of having good controls present throughout the organization. Its commitment to creating an excellent control environment (on which the management of risk will depend) must be reflected in both the resources it makes available and its attitude to those who are expected to manage risks on their behalf. This commitment must also be reflected in the funds the board makes available for technology support and the recruitment and retention of appropriately skilled resources.

Structure

Establishing leadership roles and commitment is, of course, vital, but these must be supported by the appropriate structures that provide the forums at which risks can be aired and discussed openly. These forums should be geared to the active management of particular risk categories and usually include some or all of the following: business risk management committees; operational risk management committees; credit risk management committees; and programme and project boards.

Trust

A risk management culture will not survive unless it has been built on a firm foundation of trust. Without this, risk will always be perceived as something negative. People must be given the freedom to fail. Trust at its simplest level can be defined as confidence in those on whom we depend. The achievement of this depends on:[4]

- Achieving results. First and foremost, people trust those who are willing (because of their drive, discipline and commitment) and able (because of their knowledge, skills and courage) to deliver the results they promise. By contrast, we distrust those we consider misguided or incompetent. Anyone who cannot achieve the performance expectations that our organization imposes will be hard-pressed to earn trust.

- Acting with integrity. Integrity requires honesty in one's words and consistency in one's actions. People trust those who are direct in expressing their views and predictable in acting within a known set of principles. Inconsistency suggests that leaders are dishonest or self-serving. Those who conceal or distort the truth, or who constantly change their strategies and practices, are rarely trusted. The impact of integrity is paramount early in a relationship, as each side assesses the degree to which it can trust the other.

- Demonstrating concern. Fundamentally, trust requires that leaders understand and respect the interests of people at all levels and in all constituencies. More specifically, people trust those who consider their interests even in the face of potentially conflicting pressures. This does not require leaders to place our needs above all others. We

Smart people to have on your side: Robert Galford and Anne Siebold Drapeau

Galford is a managing partner of the Center for Executive Development in Boston and Drapeau is chief people officer at Digitas, Boston. In their *Harvard Business Review* article 'The enemies of trust', they stated that, when people use the word 'trust', they refer to three different kinds:

1 strategic trust, which employees have in the leaders of their business;
2 personal trust, which employees have in their own managers; and
3 organization trust, which refers to how employees trust the organization to do the right things.

They go on to say that the enemies of trust, no matter how they are manifested, can be traced back to eight sources:

1 inconsistent messages;
2 inconsistent standards;
3 misplaced benevolence;
4 false feedback;
5 failure to trust others;
6 elephants in the parlour (pretending things don't exist);
7 rumours in a vacuum; and
8 consistent corporate underperformance.

do expect, however, that they will not deliberately take advantage of our reliance on them.

Compensation and reward mechanisms

The method through which people are compensated is another way of maintaining a risk culture. On one hand the compensation must not encourage people to take on unnecessary risks, while on the other it must reward them to take on some risk. This can be a difficult balance to strike and requires some careful design. Rewarding people on a single dimension, such as sales or profitability, will encourage predatory and risk-taking behaviours. It is far better to balance these measures with others that are less short-term in nature and force the risk taker to think of the longer-term consequences of their actions.

The creation of a healthy risk culture is designed to reduce the likelihood of shock events and minimize the incidence of irrational behaviours of key members of staff, be they on the board, working in the front office, or in control of critical safety processes and systems. Organizations that can create a culture that embraces risk and recognizes the importance of coming clean when mistakes are made will be more successful than those that can't or won't. Of course, if the risk culture is to last, it must have the ability to learn, from both success and failure, and this is the subject of the next chapter.

Smart answers to tough questions

Q. What are the benefits of a risk culture?

A. Establishing and maintaining a powerful risk culture allows organizations to:

- have full knowledge of the risks it is taking;
- trust everyone to take the right risks and avoid those that could have a significant impact on the business;
- keep risks visible;
- manage their risks appropriately and tailor their processes accordingly;
- have open and honest discussions about the risks that affect them; and
- provide an environment that allows anyone to raise critical issues without living in fear of retribution.

Notes

1   Bolger, A. (2003) 'Boardroom juggling act as dangers multiply', *Financial Times* special report, *Insurance: Risk Management*, 1 October, pp. 1–2.

2   PricewaterhouseCoopers (1999) CFO: *Architect of the Corporation's Future*, New York: John Wiley & Sons, p. 136.

3   For more information about Nedcor's approach to risk management, see www.nedcor.com.

4   Shaw, B. (1997) *Trust in the Balance*, San Francisco: Jossey-Bass.

6 Smart Thinking IV: Learn From Success and Failure

Smart quotes

Failure does not strike like a bolt from the blue; it develops gradually according to its own logic. As we watch individuals attempt to solve problems, we will see that complicated situations seem to elicit habits of thought that set failure in motion from the beginning. From that point, the continuing complexity of the task and the growing apprehension of failure encourage methods of decision making that make failure even more likely and then inevitable.

Dietrich Dörner

Warren Buffet once said, 'I often felt there might be more to be gained by studying business failures than business successes.' Business failures have more of a pattern to them than business successes. And, it's easier to generalize about failure than success.

As we saw in Chapter 5, few organizations have developed a culture where it is possible to genuinely learn from past mistakes. In such organizations, there is a general intolerance of failure and people live in fear of retribution from an autocratic, bad boss if they put a single step wrong. This inability to learn from failure is as big a problem at the individual level where, because of our own insecurities and self-beliefs, we fail to take on board the feedback and opportunity to learn that failure

Smart quotes

If we do not face up to our mistakes and accept that they happen in every job, if we are fearful of punishment, the chances are that errors will be concealed, overlooked and, in some cases, compounded.

Richard Donkin

affords. Let's face it, the majority of us pass through our life and the inevitable problems it presents blaming other people, events, bad luck, the stars, fate and indeed anything so long as it isn't ourselves. I guess that not wanting to lose face is part of the human condition and a very strong driver to ignore or dismiss failure as a one-off.

But the issue is not just about failure; it also applies to success. Few people or companies attempt to learn from success. In fact, it is probably much harder to learn from success than failure. There are a number of reasons for this, including:

Too much success can ruin you as surely as too much failure.

Marlon Brando

● success is rarely analysed;

● we overestimate our capabilities when successful;

● success is usually considered to be self-perpetuating;

● success breeds hubris; and

● success can have a detrimental effect on people's careers.

The flipside of success, failure, also presents a problem when it comes to learning, although for different, but equally important reasons, including:

- failure is usually externalized;

- any analysis is normally designed to either blame or sanitize; and

- it can be seen as a one-off event, an aberration from the norm.

In his book *The Fifth Discipline*, Peter Senge describes a number of obstacles that reduce our ability to learn at both the individual and corporate levels. The principal ones, plus my additions, are identified below.

I am my position

Failure is a great teacher.

This refers to the way we become defined by our job and how it can be very difficult to do anything else or think outside the confines of our immediate role. This tends to be reinforced by departmental (or functional) culture and the technical training people receive. In extreme cases this can be perpetuated as people move up the organization. For example, if we consider most career routes, they tend to remain within a single discipline, such as finance or information technology. This can act as a major barrier to learning and lead to blind spots in knowledge. In particular, such blind spots tend to arise at times of crisis, when stress and anxiety prevent learning (this is an automatic, physiological response of the brain, which shuts down the reasoning capability in favour of a fight or flight response).

The enemy is out there

This is a by-product of 'I am my position' and is associated with blaming others when things go wrong. This is very common in organizations where one function blames another or when a project, product or process fails. We become so embroiled in our narrowly focused roles that we fail to see the wider issues involved. As a result, we fail to learn from the experience or see the other function's or person's perspective. This ensures that we end up repeating the same mistakes time and time again. And, as already discussed, too many organizations have a blame culture that prevents learning when things go wrong. As a result, people fail to take risks because the implications of failure outweigh the benefits of going out on a limb. When things go wrong in such organizations, every effort is made to find a suitable scapegoat rather than directing energy towards the learning required to ensure the same mistake is not repeated.

The delusion of learning from experience

Increasingly, and especially within work, there is no direct link between the actions we take and the outcomes that occur. And although we learn best from direct experience, this is rarely the case within the organizational setting. To address this we must seek feedback from those around us so that we are able to learn from experience. Being a small cog in a large wheel usually limits an individual's ability to see the bigger picture and thus prevents learning. The increasing complexity of organizations is reducing our learning ability.

We fail to see the long-cycle changes

With the pace of work speeding up and our obsession with getting things done at an ever-faster rate, we often fail to see the long-term changes. Indeed, we increasingly view them as irrelevant. This is leading organizations and individuals alike to dismiss the benefits of strategy and planning. But without strategies or plans, it can be very difficult to gauge the results of actions and learn from the experience. Short-termism also affects the way people manage risks. In general, they don't.

Inaction and the knowing–doing gap

We all suffer from knowing that we should do something but failing to do it. We all avoid difficult situations, and we are all guilty of procrastination. The same applies to organizations that skirt around problems or spend endless amounts of time discussing the underlying components rather than solving them. This type of inactivity fails us all.

The word 'risk' comes from the Italian *riscare*, to dare.

Senge believes that those who are keen to learn (and hence willing to overcome their barriers to learning) must embrace the following five disciplines:

1   Personal mastery. They should continue to develop themselves personally (intellectually, emotionally and inter-personally) by setting goals and aiming to achieve them.

Smart quotes

How we see others is a huge key to the traps we set for ourselves. By casting another in a 'higher status' role to us, we automatically hand over control. In doing that we give away our responsibility and accountability. Makes life much easier. So unless the other person happens to want to let you do what you would rather be doing, you don't get to do it. But then you have someone to blame. Whereas if you take the chance and the risk yourself, you may not be prepared to take the failure. Taking risk means taking the responsibility for failure. It is not a risk without that possibility. Many a time in life we say we are taking a risk, but are not taking on the risk of failure, and are devastated when things don't work out.

Nicola Phillips

2   Mental models. They should update their mental models by removing those that are outdated and no longer suited to the modern workplace and adding new ones that are more useful. This can be done by testing existing mental models against the external environment and adjusting them as necessary.

3   Shared vision. They should be open with other people by sharing knowledge, and taking and giving feedback in order to achieve things collectively.

4   Team learning. They should work with those around them to widen their learning network and individual capabilities.

5   Systems thinking. They should understand how their organization really works, including the political and power dimensions (this is Senge's fifth discipline: being able to see patterns and systemic relationships).

Learning and feedback

The barriers identified by Senge are powerful inhibitors to learning, and the situation is further complicated by the culture of the organization. As we saw in the previous chapter, the culture of the organization

Smart quotes

Humans have an innate drive to satisfy their curiosity, to know, to comprehend, to believe, to appreciate, to develop understandings or representations of their environment and of themselves through a reflective process: the drive to learn.

Paul Lawrence and Nitin Nohria

– and even national culture – can impact how we deal with risk and failure. In the same way, it also affects our desire to learn.

However, the good news is that as human beings we are driven to learn. It is something that is ingrained in our genes; it is an innate capability. I also believe that we have the ability to pick ourselves up by our boot straps when we fail. For example, if we think of historical figures that we consider successful, we often find that, on closer inspection, they were in fact great failures before they became notable successes. Consider the following:

When failure knocks you down, will you have the guts to get up and get going, or will you give up?

- Winston Churchill was not a great scholar and failed to gain entry to Sandhurst (the military college) on two occasions and almost failed a third time; he was behind the disastrous Dardanelle's campaign in World War I; but he went on to lead Great Britain during World War II.

- Albert Einstein was a failure at school, barely made it into polytechnic and yet went on to change our thinking about the universe and was the father of the nuclear age.

The experience of great people suggests that, when we are willing to persevere and learn from failure, we can become very successful. Key to this is, of course, maintaining an openness to the learning process. We ought to find this easy because this is a skill we have had since birth. When we were young we learnt at an amazing rate, absorbing huge amounts of information. At this early stage of our development we had no choice but to fail, so we got used to experimentation and feedback. This ability remains with us as we get older, although we get a little rusty as other things get in the way such as families, work and life in general.

Everyone of us can be considered to be an informal scientist, collecting knowledge, creating models and theories. As this learning process continues throughout our lives, we accumulate a comprehensive and complex set of beliefs about ourselves and the world around us, which makes us unique. We are also willing to share our opinions, insights and ideas with those around us, which creates a kind of natural selection of ideas. Those that are useful become accepted and those that aren't fade away. The socialization of ideas depends on the process of feedback, as without it we would be unaware of what works and what doesn't and we would fail to develop in every sense of the word.

Feedback involves four very simple steps:

1   plan to do something

2   do it

3   check the outcome

4   take some action in light of the feedback.

This process is known as single-loop learning and is fine for our personal lives when we have the immediacy of feedback.

Within the workplace, this process has to be slightly different. When new employees join the organization they are gradually indoctrinated into the company culture and the collective knowledge of the business. At the same time, they bring with them their own ideas based on their past experience and will add these to the existing knowledge pool of the business they have joined. Some of the ideas will stick and alter the collective knowledge within the organization, while others will have to be dropped by the new employee. In addition, it is rare to receive such immediate feedback, because organizations are very complex and it can take time for the results of a decision or action to come through.

So, to combat this, we have to deliberately seek out feedback from those around us. This is known as double-loop learning.

A useful technique to use when soliciting feedback is the Johari Window (see Fig. 6.1). This helps to uncover those things that remain unsaid or hidden from another person. The beauty of the Johari window is that it widens our understanding of ourselves and how other people perceive us. It can also be very helpful when working in teams as, to be truly effective, there must be a lot of mutual understanding.

The four quadrants of the model are:

- Open. This is where most of us communicate. This is where those around you know what you know; in essence, what you are willing to share about yourself, your feelings, viewpoints and knowledge.

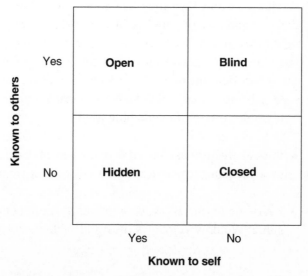

Fig. 6.1 The Johari Window

- Blind. Here, others know things about you that you are ignorant to and so they remain hidden from you. Such things tend to be behavioural in nature but, because of the nature of relationships, people are often unwilling to tell you about them. Unfortunately, these can be major inhibitors to learning and especially progression within the workplace.

- Hidden. This is the classic hidden agenda where you know something but will not pass it on to a third party. This may be what you want to achieve, or knowledge you have about an important topic and so on.

- Closed. These are things that neither you nor those around you know about you. This is the tacit knowledge and understanding that we all hold but which rarely surface.

The Johari Window can be an effective way to address the risks the organization is facing, as it will help to surface how people perceive certain risks and how they feel about them. We have to remember that the majority of people will view risks as dangerous and career-limiting events. As we have seen, this emotional association results in misunderstandings and a tendency for risks to go underground. Using the Johari Window in a risk workshop is an excellent idea and can be used to bring as many of the risks as possible into the open quadrant. This would work in the following way:

- First, all the risks associated with the venture are listed on a flipchart or whiteboard. These are the risks that are currently known.

- Everyone in the risk workshop positions each of the risks onto the Johari Window as follows (using a facilitator where appropriate):

1 Where everyone understands the risk and its consequences it is positioned in the open quadrant.
2 Where no one fully understands the risk it should be placed in the closed quadrant.
3 Where some people know what the risk is about but others do not, the risk can be placed into either the blind or hidden quadrant. To some extent it doesn't really matter because it highlights the need to develop a clearer understanding of the risk.

● Having positioned the risk, the next stage is to discuss, debate and seek closure on those risks that fall into the closed, hidden or blind quadrants in order to move them into the open quadrant. In this way a much clearer understanding of the risks can be achieved and hidden agendas can be surfaced. This ultimately improves their management and helps to establish a more productive risk culture.

● Finally, any new risks that have been identified during the process should be debated in the same way as those listed at the beginning of the workshop.

Smart voices: David Charlton[1]

David Charlton, co-founder of the Officers Club, a men's retailer and one of the UK's fastest growing companies, is convinced that the failure of his first retail venture in the early 1990s allowed him to be more successful the second time round. His first company, Fiori, also a men's retailer, failed during the early 1990s recession when the bank called in his £120,000 overdraft. A combination of a trip to Florida and his experience of running a company on an overdraft convinced him of the benefits of discount stores, which were highly successful in the US. Within six months of the first failure, Charlton had opened three Officers Club stores without any third-party support. There are now 190 stores across the country and the business turns over £100 million per year. Charlton believes that risk is a vital part of enterprise and those that have failed understand it well.

Smart voices: The US Army's After Action Review (AAR)[2]

The US Army use the AAR as means of continuous learning and improvement. The AAR originated during the Vietnam War, where the soldiers in the field knew more than those at headquarters. The AAR allows people to learn immediately after an event, irrespective of whether it was a success or failure. The key thing is that it takes place immediately. Conducting an AAR usually takes between 20 and 30 minutes and should answer the following questions:

- What should have happened?
- What actually happened?
- What were the differences between what should have and what actually happened?
- What lessons can be drawn from the experience and how can any strengths revealed be built upon, and any weaknesses reduced or eliminated?

Of course, risk management does not stop once we have identified the risks, so it is important to maintain the openness and the ability to learn as the venture continues; in other words, ensuring the risk management process is both active and adaptive. To that end I would recommend the use of the after action review (AAR) (see 'Smart voices: The US Army's After Action Review (AAR)', above). This is a great technique for soliciting immediate feedback after a key event (which may be positive as well as negative) and using this to learn lessons and apply them in future situations. As I mentioned at the beginning of this chapter, we are poor at building a clear model of what works and what doesn't. The application of techniques such as the AAR creates an environment in which it is possible to analyse both success and failure while it is still fresh in people's minds and begin to create models that can be replicated (success) and avoided or updated (failure).

Modelling success and failure

Our minds have a powerful influence over our behaviour. We have already identified that our attitude to risk has a bearing on the types of

Smart quotes

When analysing mistakes and their principal causes, there are two important lessons that should be apparent to every careful reader. First, all organizations, no matter how successful they have been or will continue to be, make mistakes ... The second lesson is equally clear: Where there is failure, there is the potential for learning. Unlike the first lesson, which is obvious to most of us, the second may be threatening. It says, in effect, that failure is not to be pushed aside, but studied. Learn from mistakes — learn how not to do it.

Kharbanda and Pinto

risk we are willing to take, be they individual or organizational. Modelling success and failure is an increasingly important skill as we navigate through a complex and confusing world. But modelling does not come easy, because each of us has built up our own set of mental models (how we interpret and react to the world around us) unconsciously. To be successful, however, we need to be far more conscious in the way we develop, use and adjust our mental models in response to the changes in our environment. This ability to model lies at the heart of neurolinguistic programming (NLP).

NLP is a relatively new concept that was derived from research into the transference of therapy skills between counsellors. The neuro (N) component of NLP states that our behaviour stems from the way we experience the world around us through our five senses. It also relates to our physiological reactions to the things we sense. The linguistic (L) element of NLP relates to the language we use to order our thoughts and behaviour, and the way we communicate with those around us. Finally, the programming (P) aspect of NLP refers to the way we, as individuals, choose to respond to the conditions around us. The application of NLP allows you to rewire the way you think about, approach and respond to events. It is therefore possible to model success and remodel failure into success using imagery in our brain.

A good example of this is how Roger Bannister managed to break the four-minute mile. Before he broke this seemingly impossible barrier no one believed it was possible, including the medical profession, which believed that the human body would not cope with the stress. Flying in the face of received wisdom, Roger built up a mental image of himself breaking the four minutes and replayed this image over and over again. By the time he came to run he knew that he was going to achieve it because he had rewired his brain for success. And, once broken, many other runners managed to come under the previously elusive four minutes, principally because they had been shown that it was possible. It was all in the mind. All sportsmen and women use a similar process and many are now working in the corporate world to transfer these skills.

Also, consider the Japanese economy (at least during the 30 years following the end of World War II). It was able to become the power-house of the global economy by modelling American and European companies and making the same products both cheaper and of a higher quality.

Modelling success and failure should therefore lie at the heart of risk management and should help change the view of risk as something dangerous to being something far more positive. It should also make all of us far more aware of what is going on around us and help us to explore why certain courses of action fail and others succeed. And, having understood why success and failure occur, we can do something about it – in other words, repeat the successes and iron out the failures. Speakers International, a company specializing in motivation and peak performance, recommend the use of the DANCE model for those who wish to model success:

- D – have a *desired* outcome

- A – take some *action*

- N – *notice* the results

- C – *change* the actions where necessary

- E – aim for *excellence*.

When this model is coupled with other techniques, such as the AAR, and existing research on failure and success, it can become even more powerful.

Dr Richard Wiseman

An award-winning professional magician, Wiseman is head of the research unit within the Psychology Department at the University of Hertfordshire, where he carries out scientific research into a range of unusual topics including the psychology of ghosts and miracles, magic, lying and intuition. He believes that luck exerts a dramatic influence over our lives and in his book *The Luck Factor*, he has developed four principles of luck:

1   maximize your chance opportunities
2   listen to your lucky hunches
3   expect good fortune
4   turn your bad luck into good.

Wiseman believes that everyone is capable of being lucky – it just requires an appropriate shift in mind-set.

A number of years ago, when I was running my first IT project, things did not go according to plan. In fact most of it went horribly wrong. Like many other people who face such a situation, I believed that most of the reasons for the failure were external – it was the users, the managers, my team and so on. At that time I was studying my Masters at the London School of Economics and decided to research into why IT projects failed. The result was a much better understanding of the dynamics of an IT project and helped me to develop a successful approach to their execution. The success of this lay in casting the re-

The key to success is preparation. I want to be part of the best team in the world. What you say to people on the pitch is not as important as everything you do before you get onto it. The image is made before the game.

Will Carling

Smart people to have on your side: John Argenti

Argenti is a business consultant and designer of the A-Score, a technique for predicting the failure of a company that consists of three categories of factors:

1 Defects:
   • autocrat
   • combined chairman and chief executive
   • passive board
   • weak finance director
   • poor management depth
   • no budgetary control
   • no cash flow plans
   • no costing system
   • poor response to change.
2 Mistakes:
   • high leverage
   • overtrading
   • big project.
3 Symptoms:
   • financial signs
   • creative accounting
   • non-financial signs
   • terminal signs.

Argenti also believes that any company failure follows three stages:

1 Crucial gaps and imbalances appear in a company's management and its internal and external monitoring systems.
2 The defects that arise in stage 1 lead to inappropriate business decisions.
3 The company shows the signs of failure, including high staff turnover and cashflow crisis.

search net very wide and building up a comprehensive model of why my own and other IT projects failed. In other words, taking the advice of Senge. More importantly, it allowed me to develop a much clearer understanding of how such projects could be made more successful and this led me to write my first book, *Failsafe IS Project Delivery*. The other thing that struck me is that organizations can learn a lot from other people's research and experience, especially when it has been distilled into the warning signs of failure, which, when flipped, become the critical factors of success (see 'Smart people to have on your side: John Argenti', p. 188). The unfortunate thing is that few people and organizations are willing to learn and few can be bothered to read or take on the lessons from research. Clearly, if we are to become more successful, this must change.

Indeed, I believe it is the ability to learn that separates the successful from the less effective among us. Too many organizations rest on their laurels, become risk averse and believe they are above learning. This leads to stagnation and an unwillingness to accept either that failure provides an opportunity to improve or that success, without understanding why, is repeatable. As we will see in Chapter 8, the ability to learn from failure lies at the heart of innovation. And innovation is not possible without risk. In the end, risk, failure and learning are related. Before we address innovation we will briefly turn to risk management and decision support, with a particular emphasis on tools and techniques.

Notes

1   Armitstead, L. (2003) 'Lessons I learnt from going bust', *Sunday Times*, 19 January, section 3, p. 13.

2   Collison, C. and Parcell, G. (2001) *Learning to Fly: Practical Lessons from one of the World's Leading Knowledge Companies*, Oxford: Capstone, pp. 76–85.

7 Risk Management and Decision Support

One of the key things to recognize about risk management is that it is inexorably linked to decision making. Throughout the entire decision-making process, risk management looms large. From considering what to do through to assessing options and taking action, we will weigh up the risks of doing something before doing it. Even if decisions are taken on the fly there will be a fleeting moment when you consider the risk. Fortunately, there are a wide range of tools and techniques that are available to support both the assessment of risk and the process of decision making.

> Ships are safest in the harbour, but that isn't what they were built for.
>
> Nicola Phillips

The purpose of this chapter is to briefly outline the nature of decision making and introduce a small number of decision support tools.

The nature of decision making

According to the University of St Thomas, the typical decision-making process follows these seven steps:

1 Define the problem that requires resolution.

2 Gather information about the problem. This will include information from stakeholders that will be affected by the decision, assess-

ing the boundaries of the problem, collating facts and figures and capturing opinions and assumptions.

3   Develop alternatives. This will involve looking at the problem from as many different perspectives as possible and may involve brainstorming, structured thinking and other techniques. Having identified the alternatives, it is then advisable to reduce these into a smaller number by combining those that are similar and eliminating those that are not viable.

4   Weigh alternatives. This will involve identifying and selecting the criteria against which the alternative courses of action will be assessed and then evaluating them. Every alternative should be assessed in terms of its suitability, feasibility and flexibility.

5   Select the best alternative. Here it is useful to consider your own intuition, seek advice and be willing to compromise.

6   Implement the solution.

7   Monitor progress.

We should, of course, remember that we are prone to bad decision making. As we saw in the early chapters of the book, few of us understand probability, many of us can over commit to bad decisions and most of us fail to fully assess risk. The foundation of such bad decision making and the escalation that usually follows lies in irrational behaviour, which encapsulates the following ten factors.

Availability error

The most recent material is available. Previous knowledge and data is lost in the immediacy of the event. Not surprisingly, this type of irrational behaviour is often stimulated by dramatic events.

> **Smart quotes**
>
> People accountable for a failed decision find themselves caught in a no-win situation: some failure is inevitable, but their superiors do not tolerate failure. Individuals in such a bind have but two options: own up, or cover up. Choosing to own up makes the day of atonement today; choosing a cover-up makes it tomorrow or perhaps never. Put in this bind, people seldom own up to failures and delay the day of atonement as long as possible. Several actions of deception are necessary to put things off. Offsetting bad news with good news deflects potentially threatening questions. The cover-up is two-tiered: the distorted good news and the blatant act of creating misleading information. These games of deception become 'undiscussable' because to reveal them would also reveal the lose-lose position created for the organization.
>
> Paul Nutt

Halo effect

The tendency to see all personal attributes consistently. For example, a good sportsman is expected to be a good businessman, father, indeed good at everything. Look at David Beckham, an icon who cannot put a foot wrong. This can equally work in the reverse, where someone is classed as being an all-round poor performer.

Primacy error

Beliefs formed by first impressions, with later evidence interpreted in light of this initial impression. The adage 'first impressions count' is applicable here and, if powerful, primacy error can generate positive or negative halo effects early on within a relationship.

Conformity error

Individual conformance to the behaviour of others, whether they know they are making a mistake by doing so, or whether they are unaware both of their mistake and of the social pressure that has induced them to make it.

Group bias

Where group members' attitudes are biased in one direction, the interaction of the group will tend to increase this bias because of the need to be valued and suppress criticism. Engaging in a common task only decreases hostility between groups if the outcome is successful. Where it is not, blame is passed from one group to the other, with any existing divisions widening.

Stereotypes

Stereotypes are convenient tools for assessing an individual who belongs to a group. As a result, rather than being expected to act individually, a member of a group is expected to conform to the stereotypical behaviour of the entire group. Therefore, no attempt is made at assessing an individual's behaviour in isolation from the rest of the group. Stereotypes tend to be self-fulfilling because of both primacy and availability errors. We should all recognize that stereotyping is a convenient tool that we use as a short cut for evaluating those around us. We stereotype people from different nations, different regions, different professions, and even our travelling companions (see, for example, the book *Pains on Trains*, which does this for the commuting population).

Public decisions

Public decisions are more likely to be executed than those taken privately. In general, people do not want to lose face, especially in public. This is a classic problem with government-sponsored projects and any initiative that involves some kind of public pronouncement by a senior executive. More than anyone else, the CEO does not want to fail.

Misplaced consistency

When you need to, can you get off the escalator?

Someone who has embarked on a course of action may feel that they must continue to justify their initial decision. People who have made a sacrifice – time, effort or money – in order to do something, tend to go on doing it even when they stand to lose more than they could gain by continuing. There is always the hope that the situation can be retrieved. This helps to explain why it can be so difficult to terminate a failing project, or pull out of a seemingly ridiculous course of action.

Ignoring the evidence

People tend to seek confirmation of their current hypothesis whereas they should be trying to dis-confirm it. In general, there is a refusal to look for contradictory evidence or, indeed, believe or act upon it if it is brought to one's attention.

Distorting the evidence

Evidence favouring a belief will strengthen it, while contradictory evidence is ignored. As a result, the belief remains intact. Therefore, when faced with evidence that is contrary to a particular viewpoint it will be distorted and dismissed as being irrelevant or inapplicable. Where the evidence is partially correct, it will be distorted to emphasize the positive aspects over the negative.

Smart people to have on your side: Helga Drummond

- Professor of Decision Sciences at the University of Liverpool, UK.
- Author of eight books, including *Escalation in Decision Making* and *The Art of Decision Making*.
- Shows how to avoid overcommitment to a failing course of action.
- Believes that it is easier to get into a mess than get out of it.

Decisions, if they are to be effective, need to be based on accurate, timely and useful information, which can range from historical costs, economic trends (both past and current), competitor information, market data, prices, current operating performance and so on. Unsurprisingly, with so much technology swilling around organizations there is a wide range of sources of data that can be drawn upon and modelled in order to assess the numerous risks faced by the typical business. But beware: if the information is incorrect or out of date, the results can be worse than if there were no information at all. So, if you are going to use a mass of data when contemplating your decision, be sure to check that it is reliable and, ideally, captured from a single and reliable source.

The smart use of tools and techniques ensures that those taking decisions can avoid many of the cognitive biases mentioned in Chapter 1 as well as the particular problem of overestimating their capabilities (see 'Smart people to have on your side: Dan Lovallo and Daniel Kahneman', p. 197). Avoiding the natural biases we have involves:

- viewing situations from different perspectives, not just the one that you believe is the most obvious or relevant;

- being willing to examine and test assumptions, rather than accepting them blindly;

- examining the motivations of a decision, especially when already committed to a course of action;

- seeking additional and perhaps expert input before committing to a decision; and

- accepting that your ego can get in the way.

Smart people to have on your side: Dan Lovallo and Daniel Kahneman

Dan Lovallo is a senior lecturer at the Australian Graduate School of Management at the University of New South Wales and Daniel Kahneman is Eugene Higgins Professor of Psychology at Princeton University. In their article 'Delusions of success: How optimism undermines executive decisions',[1] they state that the high failure rate of major investment projects and decisions is not the result of rational choices gone wrong, but rather a consequence of flawed decision making and over-optimism. Lovallo and Kahneman believe that such over-optimism can be traced back to cognitive bias and organizational pressures. For example, people will often exaggerate their own talents and the degree of control they have over events. Such over-optimism is exacerbated by anchoring (any decision always has a starting point, or anchor, against which new information is considered), competitor neglect and organizational pressure (due to limited resources). In order to avoid such problems, they suggest that organizations should adopt what they term the outside view, which entails:

1   Selecting a reference class that is similar to the initiative being assessed. This must be statistically significant if it is to provide the information required to assess the new initiative.
2   Assessing the distribution of outcomes. This involves taking the outcomes (both successful and unsuccessful) of past projects, which will be used to assess the new initiative.
3   Making an intuitive prediction of the project's position in the distribution. This involves thinking about the expected outcome of the new initiative and then placing it along the distribution. At this stage it is highly likely that the position will be optimistic. To correct this, Lovallo and Kahneman recommend the next two steps.
4   Assessing the reliability of the prediction. This involves estimating the correlation between the forecast outcome and the actual outcome, using the distribution of prior projects. This is expressed as a number between 0 (no correlation) and 1 (complete correlation).
5   Correcting the intuitive estimate. This involves bringing the forecast outcome of the new initiative towards the average of the outcomes of the prior projects. How much of an adjustment depends on the assessment of reliability made in the previous step. Where this was unreliable, the movement is greater.

Some tools and techniques

Rather than describing highly specialized decision support tools, or attempting to detail the inner workings of software packages, I have concentrated on a small number of techniques that organizations find useful. These have a general application and share a simplicity that should allow anyone to use them. Naturally, there are others and I would recommend you explore the full range of tools available to you. The techniques are:

- *Scenario planning*, which is one of the best ways to identify the strategic risks an organization might face, especially those that could arise over the long term.

- *Decision trees*, which can be used to assess the implications of alternative decisions and are suited to situations that involve making financial or number-based decisions.

- *Monte Carlo simulation*, which is useful for conducting sensitivity analysis and testing the impact of changing variables on the outcome of a decision.

- *SWOT analysis*, which is an excellent way to assess the internal and external dynamics of the organization, especially in relation to strategy.

- *Forcefield analysis*, which is another method for considering the pros and cons of a particular decision.

- *Influence modelling*, which allows an organization to capture and model the way its business and the markets in which it operates work and, through this, understand how a decision about one factor can impact others.

- *Portfolio analysis*, a technique developed by the Boston Consulting Group, which allows an organization to assess how well its products, services and business units are faring in the marketplace. This information can then be used to direct investment decisions.

Scenario planning

Scenario planning is an increasingly popular tool for attempting to understand the future and what it might mean for the organization in terms of the risks it might face and how it might respond. Rather than beginning with the present and projecting forward, scenario planning starts with the future and projects back to the present.

The attractiveness of this technique is that it provides the basis for creative thinking. It does this by building consensus on the likely futures the organization will face and helps to sensitize senior executives to the risks associated with each scenario. It is also a very useful way of testing the robustness of any strategy as, once established, it is possible to play any strategy against each of the scenarios to test whether or not it will hold up under different circumstances. It must be recognized that developing scenarios takes time because it requires a significant amount of research into the factors that are affecting the future. Therefore, if scenario planning is going to be used, it is best incorporated into the strategic planning process.

Smart people to have on your side: Palisade Corporation

- Leader in the decision analysis software industry.
- Supplies software tools to executives and academics in the area of risk and decision analysis.
- Has developed a range of software tools to support strategic, business, financial and project risk management.
- Has published a number of books that describe the application and use of its tools.
- More information can be found at www.palisade.com.

When creating scenarios, most companies use the following categories of factors:

- Demographics, including the ageing of the population, immigration, shifting patterns of population within countries and so on.

- Environmental change, which is increasingly important for many companies and includes such things as pollution, global warming, depletion of natural resources and so on.

- Economics.

- Science and technological change, including trends such as biotechnology and information technology.

- Government and international legislation and control.

- Customers, their behaviours and expectations.

- Competitors and how they impact the market(s) in which the company operates.

- People in general, in terms of their attitudes and behaviours.

The analyses of these and other trends allow the organization to develop a number of scenarios or future worlds in which it will have to exist and hence adapt to. Scenarios use combinations of the identified factors and trends and serve to describe, not predict, the future using a small number of key drivers. These drivers are derived from the analysis of the trends and factors and are usually binary in nature (see 'Smart voices: Royal Institute of International Affairs (RIIA)', below).

Smart voices: Royal Institute of International Affairs (RIIA)

The Royal Institute of International Affairs has developed scenarios for 2020. In generating the scenarios, the RIIA has considered a global backdrop in which there will be around 4 billion poor people (who currently create less than 1 per cent of world product), 2 billion aspirants (who create around 14 per cent of world product) and over 1 billion citizens of the wealthy nations (who create over 85 per cent of world product). The RIIA believes that the world of 2020 will face some resource shortages – with fresh water a prime issue in some areas – but the central environmental concern will be the management of pollutant sinks, with local and transnational implications. In developing the scenarios, the RIIA considered three areas:

- commerce
- the public sector
- private lives.

Two scenarios have been developed.

Pushing the edge

In this scenario, there is a glow of prosperity across the world, particularly in the US. Science and commerce continue to expand and innovate, and governments adopt a laissez-faire attitude. However, by 2010 problems begin to emerge from two sources. First, there are problems associated with an ageing society and poor pension provision, particularly in Europe and Japan, which in turn makes it difficult for these people to accommodate continuous technological change. Second, problems stem from the inability of institutions to deal with increasing and sophisticated regulations. From 2010 to 2020 the major economies find themselves at odds politically and unable to cope with the high levels of change. No one is paying attention to the poor, there are increasing problems over the theft of intellectual property, the world becomes a dangerous place and the lack of environmental concern leads to stress and conflict.

Renewed foundations

There is limited economic growth from 2000 onward due to the problems in the Old Economy, and the flood of cheap goods and services from low-wage countries has commoditized entire industries. At the same time, the New Economy is failing to deliver on its promises and, although producing new products, it does not generate much profit. The public sector is consuming around half of all added value, with the majority being directed into welfare. The elderly worry about their assets, and state support is inadequate. Companies begin to engage in irregular activities, mainly outside regulatory control and within the poorer nations. The use of knowledge allows nations to improve the skills of their workers and increase the level of collaboration. Communities fade and as a consequence there is a greater dependence on the state. In response to its inability to provide what people are looking for, many start to focus on the electronic media as a means of connecting with those with the same opinions and attitudes. Over time, such bottom-up collaboration leads to increasing activism and the emergence of a micro-democracy, which ties together industry and consumer, private and public sectors. By 2020 this bottom-up integration is still incomplete.

Here are some of the rules that should be applied if the scenarios produced are to be valuable:

- At least two scenarios should be developed, as one would not be sufficient to model the uncertainties.

- They must be plausible. If they are too off the wall, no one will relate to them and they will be destined to become shelfware.

- They must relate to the organization's operating and market environments. If the scenario describes something that is unrelated to the business, it will not have the desired impact on creativity or thinking.

Each scenario has a theme and a name that people can readily understand (for example, 'Caring Corporates') and each major factor (technology, economy, government and so on) is described within the scenario's theme. The implications on the organization are also identified, although at this stage they are usually at a high level. Once a more detailed strategy has been developed it is normally tested against each of the scenarios, which helps to assess its robustness under a variety of contexts. It also helps to prepare the organization for the uncertain times ahead.

The value of scenarios is usually illustrated by Shell, which used them to predict and then manage the impacts of the 1970s oil crisis. Shell's development of scenarios involved their operational managers, who had to describe how they would respond to the futures provided to them during their long-term planning process. As a result, Shell was able to respond much faster than its competitors during the oil crisis. Over the years Shell has benefited from scenario planning in five ways:

1   It found that its strategic decisions and project investments were more robust under different futures, thereby future-proofing them.

2   It became much better at thinking about the future.

3   Its manufacturing personnel became more perceptive and able to recognize events as being part of a pattern, rather than as isolated incidents.

4   The company was able to set a wider context for decision making down the line instead of dictating precise and direct instructions.

5   The company was able to use scenarios as a leadership tool.

How good is your decision making?

After more than 25 years of scenario planning, Shell would not manage its strategic risks any other way. Scenario planning is increasingly popular within government and military circles and is gradually taking hold within industry, although very slowly because of the time it takes to produce results; something that fast-paced CEOs just haven't got time for – they need tomorrow's solution the day before yesterday, not in three months' time. The smart organization will understand the value of scenarios and will use them where appropriate.

Monte Carlo simulation

This approach is named after the roulette wheels in Monte Carlo, which are considered to be mechanisms for generating random numbers. The technique was originally developed for the Manhattan Project during World War II, which led to the development of the atomic bomb. These days the technique is applied to more peaceful and wide-ranging problems, such as stock market forecasting and designing nuclear reactors.

The method randomly selects values to create scenarios for a given problem. The values are taken from a fixed range and are selected to fit a particular probability distribution, such as the normal distribution. The simulation involves repeating the selection process many times in order to create multiple scenarios. Each of the scenarios represents one possible outcome and hence one possible solution to the problem. When repeated thousands of times it is possible to build up a picture of all the possible outcomes across the distribution and the more times the simulation is run, the more accurate the result. Creating a Monte

Carlo simulation for a business investment or problem involves four steps:

1   To begin with it is necessary to develop a cashflow model for the investment or business model under analysis. This involves capturing information about inputs, such as costs (fixed and variable), sales, interest rates and prices, and outputs, such as revenues, annual cash flows and rates of return. The cashflow model is usually built into a spreadsheet for ease of use.

2   Having identified the inputs and outputs, it is necessary to model the uncertainties of the key inputs using a probability distribution based on historic data, expert opinion, scenario analysis or management opinion. This essentially shows how the value of the input variable changes across the selected distribution, be it normal or skewed.

3   Next, it is necessary to identify the relationships between the input variables. With the operating environments of most businesses being highly complex, it is rare to find that the variables are independent of each other (see the section on influence modelling, p. 211–13).

4   Finally, the simulation is run. This involves selecting samples of the input variables across the probability distributions, calculating the outputs and presenting these as a probability distribution.

Smart quotes

Sensitivity analysis can be used by testing individual assumptions rather than changing several assumptions at once ... The differences in results thrown up will illustrate the riskiness of a particular plan.

James Morrell

Decision trees

Decision tress can be useful in a number of circumstances, including those that involve assessing a large number of factors and those in which there is a large number of alternative decisions that need to be explored. They provide a useful structure in which it is possible to lay out and evaluate alternative decisions and the implications of those decisions. They are especially useful in assessing the risks and opportunities associated with a particular choice. Developing a decision tree involves the following steps (see Fig. 7.1 for a completed tree):

- First, it is necessary to start with the decision that is to be made. On the tree, this is represented by a square on the left-hand side of the diagram.

- Straight lines are drawn from the square box, each representing one possible solution.

- At the end of each solution line consider the result: if it is uncertain, draw a circle (which represents uncertainty); if another decision has to be made, draw another square. Write the decision above the square and the factor above the circle.

- From the new squares and circles draw lines representing the options that could be taken and their possible outcomes.

- If you have reached a solution (i.e. at the end of the line there are no further squares or circles), draw a triangle (which represents the point where a defined outcome has been arrived at).

- Continue the process until you have exhausted the possible outcomes and decisions.

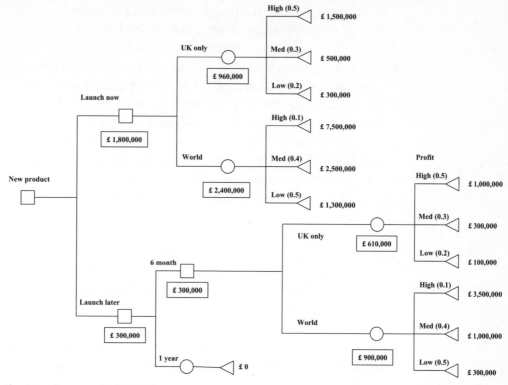

Fig. 7.1   An example decision tree

- Having completed the diagram, review each square and circle to ensure you have covered every possible decision and outcome and revise the tree if necessary.

- Having reviewed and finalized the diagram, it is necessary to start the process through which you can determine the optimum decision, which usually means the one that provides the best financial return.

- A monetary value should be assigned to each of the triangles. This is what the outcome is worth to you. The value should be realistic and, when arriving at the figure, you might consider input from other sources, be they internal, historical or external.

- A probability value should now be assigned to each of the lines that come out from the circles. All the lines from a single circle should, when added together, equal 100 per cent (or 1 in probability terms). Therefore, if you believe that of three options associated with a particular outcome the first has a 30 per cent chance of occurring and the second a 50 per cent chance, the final one should have a 20 per cent chance. These options would be represented as 0.3, 0.5 and 0.2 respectively. Where appropriate use historical data or the advice of experts.

- Once you have determined the outcomes and assessed their probabilities, it is time to calculate the values that will help you arrive at a decision. To do this, begin at the right-hand side of the tree and work back towards the original decision.

- As you complete a set of calculations for each circle and square, record the result. All the calculations that lead to the result can be ignored from now on (this is termed 'pruning').

- When dealing with the circles it is necessary to calculate the total value for the outcome by multiplying the value you assigned to each triangle by the probability you assigned to the line and adding the results together.

- When addressing the decision node (the squares) write down the cost of each option down the decision line and subtract this from the value of the outcome (which you previously derived). This will give you the expected benefit if you chose that decision. The decision with the highest benefit should be chosen.

SWOT analysis

SWOT analysis is a very simple tool that allows you to identify the strengths, weaknesses, opportunities and threats of a particular venture, situation or project (see Fig. 7.2). The value of the technique is that it ensures there is a balanced assessment by focusing on the upside (strengths and opportunities) as well as the downside (weaknesses and threats). Carrying out a SWOT analysis usually involves a small number of people in a workshop environment. The purpose is to answer questions such as:

- What are the competitive advantages of the organization?

- What does the company do well?

- What could be improved?

- What is not done as well as it should be?

- What should the company avoid?

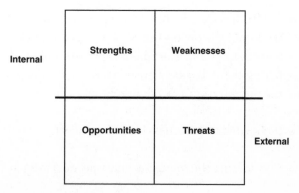

Fig. 7.2 SWOT analysis

- Where do the future opportunities lie?

- What else could the business do?

- What obstacles does the business face?

- What is the competition doing?

- What is happening in the wider economy and markets?

- How is technology changing?

- How are the company's finances?

Answering these questions, with suitable debate, allows everyone to gain a better understanding of the factors that need to be considered when a critical decision is being made. As expected, the types of question that should be asked will vary according to the nature of the decision. SWOT analysis can be used for:

- The strategic assessment of an organization.

- Determining areas that the organization needs to develop. This can be done by viewing the SWOT analysis internally (strengths and weaknesses) and externally (opportunities and threats) and comparing the two sets of answers. Any areas of poor fit will feed into the organization's development.

- Reviewing the business case of a project.

- Considering the merits of a new product launch.

Forcefield analysis

Forcefield analysis is a tool that is particularly useful when dealing with change. The idea behind it is that rather than increase the forces for the change it is often useful to reduce those that oppose it. To do so requires the organization to get a complete view of all the forces that support or oppose the change so that a decision can be made which takes into account all interests. Carrying out a forcefield analysis involves:

- Listing all the forces for and against the change.

- Scoring each of the forces from 1 (weak) to 5 (strong).

- Drawing a diagram that summarizes each of the forces and therefore provides an indication of whether the change will be successful (see Fig. 7.3).

The decisions we make today impact our organization tomorrow.

- Developing strategies for improving the likelihood of success through the reduction in the opposing forces.

Influence modelling

Influence modelling is a technique that allows an organization to capture and summarize how its business functions and how this relates to the dynamics of the market(s) in which it works. The modelling is normally conducted in a workshop environment and involves:

- Establishing the factors that can impact/drive the business.

- Creating the links between these factors.

- Understanding how one factor influences another.

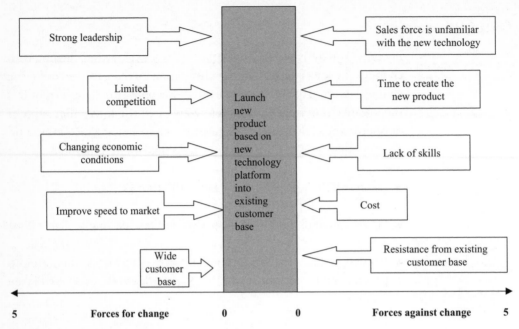

Fig. 7.3 Forcefield analysis

Having developed the basic model, it is calibrated through data analysis and input from other parties within and, potentially, outside the organization. The final step in the process is to replicate the model in something like Excel or a business intelligence package so that it can be used in the decision-making process. The model can be used to:

● Test decisions under a variety of different scenarios.

● Capture the wider and often systemic impacts of a decision.

● Understand the risks associated with a decision.

One of the major benefits of this technique is the consensus it builds across an organization. This is principally down to the need to involve a wide range of stakeholders during the development of the model. The process of model development also helps to highlight any misconceptions, hidden opinions and blind spots (as in the Johari Window discussed in Chapter 6) and through this creates a shared understanding of what makes the business function the way it does, what its strengths are and, most importantly, where it weaknesses lie (see Fig. 7.4).

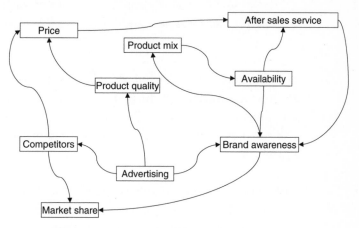

Fig. 7.4 Example of influence modelling

Portfolio analysis

Portfolio analysis allows organizations to understand the relationships between market share, cash generation and the products and services it sells. The approach is based on three concepts:

- The product life cycle – in essence, a product will emerge, grow, mature and eventually decline.

- The experience curve, which states that, as the cumulative historical output of the firm increases, unit costs fall, thereby creating dynamic economies of scale.

- Portfolio matrices, of which the most popular is the Boston Consulting Group's growth–share matrix, which allows companies to assess their products, services and business units in terms of the growth rate of the industry and the relative market share of their offerings. This allows them to classify these as being a dog (low growth and low market share); a cash cow (low growth rate and high market share); a star (high growth and high market share); or a problem child (high growth and low market share). The idea is that any business should have an appropriate mix of star, cash cow and problem child products, services and businesses if it is to have a long-term future.

Portfolio analysis is relatively straightforward to execute and can help the business track its products and services over time. Like other tools mentioned in this chapter, its purpose is to help identify the areas of risk and opportunity and, through this, to inform the decision-making process.

Risk management is an integral part of the decision-making process. But to avoid the obvious problems of excessive optimism or pessimism, the use of decision support tools and techniques, such as those introduced in this chapter, help to establish an appropriate balance between risk and reward. This in turn should help organizations back those initiatives that will lead to the best returns and avoid those that could turn out to be failures. Of course, this is not always possible because irrational behaviours can get in the way. This ability to select the best investment and balance risk and reward is especially important when it comes to innovation. And it is to this that we now turn.

Notes

1   Lovallo, D. and Kahneman, D. (2003) 'Delusions of success: How optimism undermines executive decisions', *Harvard Business Review*, July, pp. 56–63.

8 Risk Management and Innovation

In search of the silver bullet

One does not discover new continents without consenting to lose sight of the shore for a very long time.

André Gide

Academics, organizations, gurus and consultants alike have spent vast sums of money and expended huge amounts of effort to find the silver bullet that will lead to a long, successful and near risk-free corporate existence. Unfortunately, none have succeeded. The notion that a single idea, such as business process re-engineering, customer relationship management or organizational culture, will provide a risk-free future is counter-intuitive and is something that is not reflected in experience. And yet, time and again business leaders will lap it up in the hope that it will provide them and their organization with long-term competitive advantage with only the minimum of outlay and commitment.

Isn't it about time you stopped searching for the answer and took a risk to find it out for yourself?

The silver bullet syndrome is the term applied to the seeking out and acceptance of a single-shot solution to a complex business problem. Silver bullet solutions are, by their very nature, inherently seductive because they provide senior executives with a straightforward method of resolving a hard-to-crack and usually risky business problem. Under intense pressure to improve operational efficiencies and increase competitive advantage, managers will grab at anything that, according to those who peddle them, is capable of solving their business problems – often without too much difficulty.

This focus on a 'one size fits all' approach to management is nothing new. Indeed, management fads have descended on the business community with such ferocity over the last two to three decades that it's no wonder senior executives just do not know which way to turn. Management theory, be it of the 'in search of excellence' genre, total quality management, business process re-engineering, Japanese management, empowerment, human resource management, self-managed teams, customer relationship management and, latterly, knowledge management, is pervasive. Each new theory professes to provide the organization with the tools and wherewithal to achieve competitive advantage. There may of course be some short-term gain in adopting the latest management technique, but there is rarely the long-term advantage or organizational longevity that is hoped for. Adopt Japanese management and it will be possible to replicate the success of the post-war Japanese economy – but who wants to emulate the Japanese, given their recent economic difficulties? 'Don't automate, obliterate' came the war cry from the business process re-engineering gurus – downsizing, misery and a subsequent fear of failure was the response from corporate America. The New Economy is the only economy, said the dotcomers; a few short months later, they were asking for their jobs back in the Old Economy.

The history of management theory is littered with failed catch-all solutions. The gurus will say that these are the result of failing to implement them properly (maybe), but they are also due to the way in which the gurus distil a complex problem into a simple, single model and then peddle this to the desperate business community – made all the more desperate by what they read in the press, academic journals and books, often, it has to be said, written by the gurus.

Perhaps managers should be forgiven for making the mistake of believing that each new management theory will be the one that provides them with the success they are seeking. But in believing there is one best way, they feed the theorists and peddlers of such approaches.

Smart people to have on your side: Eileen Shapiro

- President of the Hillcrest Group Inc.
- Author of *Fad Surfing in the Boardroom*.
- Defines fad surfing as 'the practice of riding the crest of the latest management wave and then paddling out again just in time to ride the next one; always absorbing for managers and lucrative for consultants; frequently disastrous for organizations.'
- Believes that CEOs should have the courage to manage consciously and actively rather than running on autopilot, which permits them to avoid applying their independent judgement.

Moreover, when a particular theory fails to live up to its expectations it is secretly buried or rejected as being unsuitable. The organization will typically seek out the next silver bullet, with equal fervour and, it should be said, with equally patchy results. Unfortunately this cycle of adoption, failure and rejection is repeated many times over without ever finding success. This also subjects the organization to a constant tirade of change, the majority of which is pointless and possibly self-defeating – often termed as going-through-the-motions; no one is really bought into the change beyond the superficial compliance expected by management. There is never any long-term commitment required to make the innovation a success. The belief that an organization and its internal and external environments can be distilled into a few simple models is missing the point by a very wide margin. The business environment is complex, and this requires a complex organization to be able to respond to it.

It would be far safer, sensible and more profitable to dismiss a do-nothing director and to put a bag of sand in his chair.

Herbert Casson

If we accept that organizations are unlikely to survive in perpetuity and that there are no silver bullets that are capable of providing the longevity they seek, what can managers do? First of all they must be willing to embrace uncertainty. It is clear that no one is capable of navigating the future with pure certainty, which means that there will be many occasions when they have to take a risk or two. Therefore, to be successful over the medium to long term, business leaders should become smarter at how they identify and manage their risks. Of course, being expert at managing risk will not, on its own, secure the future of any company. But unlike the quick-fix solutions, risk management is distinguished by the need to accept and embrace complexity and deal with an environment that cannot be distilled into a simple model or managed through a guru-driven silver bullet.

But, as we have seen in earlier chapters, there seems to be a pervasive air of risk aversion hanging over us all; whether we are seeking to take risks within organizations or on our own, we appear to be constantly taking the easy option and one in which perceived risks are in fact not risks at all. We seem to be in some kind of stasis where we either stick our heads in the sand and ignore the risks around us or believe that every minor risk is a major one. This is a major problem insofar as it prevents us from being truly innovative. And it is only through innovation that we can make a difference, develop new products and create new opportunities.

For a long time now, organizations have been opting for incremental change rather than attempting to take a radical departure from the status quo. This has led to businesses seeking growth through acquisitions rather than new product development and is one of the reasons why the 1990s boom was built on sand; there were plenty of mergers but little innovation. The former were short cuts to gaining market share or the order books of competitors, but it did not result in the creation of new products. As a result, there is little new that is driving our future wealth. Innovation takes time and is a risky affair. But it lies at the heart of risk management and, more importantly, successful organizations.

Innovation

A year or so ago, I was asked to edit a book, *The Innovation Wave*, which, as the title suggests, was all about how innovation can be allowed to

Smart quotes

… innovation cannot just be 'unleashed', like some kind of frustrated dog that has not been out of the house for a while. The saying that inspiration is 99 per cent perspiration is probably closer to the truth. The people who genuinely innovate tend to be those who have trained in a specialist field, have full knowledge of past achievements, and toil and experiment over a long period of time. This is not elitist. It simply recognises that genuine insights that advance knowledge tend to come out of this process, not from people suddenly attempting to use the 'left side of their brain'.

Benjamin Hunt

succeed in organizations. It struck me that, like most other aspects of organizational life, it was a complex process but, unlike most, it required an exceptional ability to manage risk. This means that if an organization is going to innovate, and hence grow and expand, it must be willing and able to manage the inherent risks that come with it. Innovation is never without risk. If it were, there would be no modernization. Let's face it, we are all capable of originality and many of us have had brilliant ideas that we have never followed through. The problem is that turning an inspirational idea into a tangible outcome is hard and something that many of us do not attempt because we are worried about failing. In other words, we feel that the risks are too great. Such risks include:

The fastest way to succeed is to double your failure rate.

Thomas Watson Snr

- Somebody else might steal the idea – I have seen many people who are too protective of their ideas to allow them to be appropriately socialized and turned into new products and concepts.

- No one will take it, or you, seriously – unfortunately, we are often too embarrassed to talk about ideas because of the fear of failure; we dismiss the idea before we even give it a chance to succeed. Similarly, there are always plenty of people to rubbish ideas because of the not-invented-here attitude of colleagues and senior management.

- It will take too much time and investment – with increased pressure to produce near-immediate results, many organizations are stifling their ability to develop new products.

- There are too many other things vying for your attention, which prevents you from spending as much time as you need to make the idea fly.

- If it was worth doing, any one of the major companies would have already done it – this is always a great excuse not to develop first-mover advantage.

But overcoming these natural risks is possible. After all, had everyone used any of the reasons above for not pursuing a new idea, we would not have any of the things we take for granted in our lives, such as the telephone (invented by Alexander Graham Bell in 1876), the television (invented by John Logie Baird in 1926) and the aeroplane (invented by the Wright Brothers in 1903), and we certainly would not have such high levels of computerization in the workplace. Even at a much more local level, we can make a difference by going out on a limb and running with an idea. And, so what if it fails? At the very least you will have experienced something new and would have learnt something along the way. I think we are all just a little bit too anal at times, especially when faced with a an idea that looks exciting. Instead of going for it and taking a risk, we spend more time thinking about how it could fail rather than understanding why it could succeed. Many of us hold back because our leaders cannot, or will not, accept failure. Until this changes, few people will innovate of their own accord – well, not within the work setting (see 'Smart people to have on your side: Richard Farson and Ralph Keyes', p. 223).

Smart people to have on your side: Richard Farson and Ralph Keyes

Richard Farson is co-founder and president of the Western Behaviour Sciences Institute in La Jolla, California, and author of *Management of the Absurd: Paradoxes in Leadership*; Ralph Keyes is the author of *Chancing It: Why We Take Risks* and *The Courage To Write: How Writers Transcend Fear.*

In their book *Whoever Makes The Most Mistakes Wins: The Paradox Of Innovation* and their *Harvard Business Review* article 'The failure-tolerant leader', Farson and Keyes explain that, although there is a growing acceptance of failure in businesses and that this is changing the way organizations approach innovation, the story is very different at the individual level, because no one likes to fail.

They assert that it is a fault-tolerant leader who helps people overcome their fear of failure and through this creates a culture of intelligent risk taking. The fault-tolerant leader sends a clear message to the organization that mistakes are worthwhile, which in turn ensures employees no longer think in terms of success and failure but in terms of learning and experience.

So we can safely say that innovation is important. But how do organizations balance the need to manage their risks with the need to innovate? The movie business is a good example. Around 60 per cent of all films fail to generate enough ticket sales to cover their production costs. They are flops. Comparatively few become blockbusters. But it is the blockbusters that make the money. Because there are so few blockbusters, the film industry has to continually search for the latest idea that could capture the imagination of the film-going public. Key to this is searching out and using the latest technologies. For example, *The Matrix* was the first film to use bullet time, which allowed the actions of the main characters, such as Neo, to be played out in near-frozen time. This was achieved by using banks of hundreds of cameras synchronized to photograph the movements of the actors as they played out the scene. When combined with the normal motion picture the producers were able to create some amazing effects, such as speeding bullets slowed right down so that you could see their every movement.

Similarly, the latest *Lord of the Rings* film, *The Return of the King*, involves computer technology and the animation of horses, men and orcs to recreate some of the largest battle scenes ever seen on film. Indeed, computers and special effects hold the key to these and many of the other bestselling films, such as *Shrek* and *Monsters Inc*. What is clear is that any major film requires significant investment in terms of both time and money, often hundreds of millions of dollars – all this without any guarantee of any return. For example, Kevin Costner's *Waterworld* cost hundreds of millions to make and was a flop. Increasingly the film industry is seeking to reduce its risks by making sequels to blockbusters. It seems that if a film works once then it ought to work many times over. Although this may not reduce the production costs, it does reduce the risk of it failing at the box office.

If you are going to take risks, you need courage.

Coming back to the typical organization rather than the film industry, it is those with entrepreneurial sprit that are the catalysts of innovation and change. It is the visionary leader, or the engineer, beavering away on a new theory that are the true builders and dreamers of business. These are the people that have the courage of their convictions despite the scepticism of those around them. These are the people who are prepared to accept and embrace the risks because they know in return that they will secure the rewards and profits of their endeavours. Such entrepreneurs are also willing to challenge the establishment and break through the natural resistance that ensures the status quo is maintained. This combination of intellectual flare and courage is very rare in organizations.

Smart quotes

If history teaches anything about business, it is entrepreneurship thrives in a supportive culture, but that entrepreneurship is a combination of risk, motivation, and intelligence that coincides in only one manager in ten, at best. Rather than teaching entrepreneurship to the masses, we should be looking for ways at identifying entrepreneurial potential and then encouraging and supporting that potential. In that process, all managers have a role to play; we should become capable of spotting entrepreneurs even if we don't have their abilities. Let us study history, not so that we can become entrepreneurs, but so that we can learn to recognize entrepreneurship when we see it.

Morgen Witzel

So, what factors help establish an environment that supports innovation? According to Bettina von Stamm of the London Business School, they include the following:[1]

- Accepting failure as part of the innovation process.

- Linking the development of new products to the organization's strategy.

- Balancing risky and less risky projects.

- Using multifunctional teams.

- Creating reward systems that encourage entrepreneurial behaviours.

- Ensuring senior management buy into the importance of innovation.

Part of the art of fostering innovation and helping the business to grow is being able to spot those new products and ideas that are going to make a difference. For some organizations this can prove to be difficult because they have so many ideas that it can be hard to identify those that will succeed. And, of course, there are those companies that have no ideas at all. I know which problem I would like to have. According to Pearson, author of *Managing Innovation: An Uncertainty-reducing Process*, success in managing innovation depends on how the risks of innovation are controlled. He believes that if the level of uncertainty could be defined, the potential problems could be pre-empted and hence managed more effectively. By comparing the uncertainty of output against uncertainty about the process he produced an uncertainty map:

- Where uncertainty about the output and uncertainty about the process are both high, he recommends an approach that involves exploratory research. In this instance, everything is up for grabs.

- Where both uncertainty dimensions are low, he recommends a technical market combination; in other words, given that the product is likely to succeed and the process is well defined, a tried and tested approach is the best way to approach innovation. In essence, painting by numbers.

- Where the uncertainty about the process is high and the uncertainty about the output low, development engineering is the way to manage the innovation process. Here, new processes have to be developed to meet the needs of the new product, which is likely to succeed.

- Where the uncertainty about the process is low and uncertainty about the output is high, Pearson recommends an applications engineering approach. Here, the focus is building on and applying standard approaches for product development but taking greater care in testing whether the product will succeed.

Smart voices: Kraft[2]

In response to the increased concerns about obesity and the link to food producers, Kraft has taken action to cut the size of its portions and reduce the fat and sugar content of its products. This is a significant move by one of the world's largest food producers (products include Philadelphia cheese and Suchard chocolate) that will undoubtedly put pressure on its competitors, such as Unilever, Nestlé and Cadbury Schweppes. Although not publicly stated, it has been argued that Kraft has recognized the potential risks of maintaining the status quo when the likelihood of litigation is growing. The company is setting up a committee to advise on obesity and will work with it to establish appropriate portion sizes. In addition, it is dropping the marketing of its products in schools, reviewing which of its products find their way into school vending machines and including nutritional information on its food labels.

Research by the Department of Trade and Industry in the UK found that only about 10 per cent of all businesses could be considered growth firms, where their leaders were willing to take the risks associated with expansion. The rest were in steady state, where the business had reached a level of income and profitability that was satisfactory. In this case, companies are willing to limit their growth in return for lower risk.[3] For those organizations that have settled down to a dull but consistent existence there is a pressing need to challenge the sacred cows – the beliefs and values that are held dear by the organization and its leaders.

Part of the problem with innovation may be down to the business leaders of such staid companies finding it difficult to respond to disruptive innovations – technologies or business models that allow companies to offer cheaper and simpler products and services compared to those that currently exist. Response is difficult because the new services and products tend to appeal to new and low-end customers whom the business is not willing to serve. The Internet was a disruptive technology that caused major problems for the bricks-and-mortar companies but also sustained

Smart people to have on your side: Peter Drucker

According to management guru Peter Drucker in his book *Innovation and Enterprise*, innovation within business rarely springs from a flash of inspiration; rather, it arises from a cold-eyed analysis of seven kinds of opportunity:

1   Unexpected occurrences – these can mean unexpected opportunity, as well as unexpected failure, if only organizations paid attention to them. Dramatic departures from anticipated results can lead to insights, which in turn drive innovation.

2   Incongruities – these might exist between assumptions and events, expectations and results, and incongruity between economic realities. All types of incongruity open up possibilities and stimulate action to bring things back into alignment.

3   Process needs – processes drive many things, including our work-based activities and the need for effective and efficient processes can force organizations to innovate, especially when the processes are poor.

4   Industry and market changes – any significant change in the dynamics and structure of a market provides ample opportunity for innovation. Such innovation is often restricted to the new entrants, at least for the short to medium term, as it takes the established players some time to respond.

5   Demographic changes – this area is arguably one of the most consistent predictors of innovation. For example, as population dynamics change so do the markets that serve them and, as a consequence, new products and services have to be developed by those businesses that wish to remain competitive.

6   Changes in perception – very often the *glass is half empty* is a great spur for innovation because it ensures that businesses do not rest on their laurels. If we look at any organization that has been forced to innovate and change it has often been because of the perception that they were invincible and did not need to change.

7   New knowledge – the majority of innovations do not arise from a single piece of knowledge, they occur because of new knowledge being combined with that which already exists, or from the accumulation of knowledge over a longer time period. Such a convergence of knowledge can take decades.

such businesses as Dell and Amazon. The important point here, and one that is spelt out by Clayton Christensen in his book *The Innovator's Dilemma*, is that an innovation can be both disruptive and sustaining.[4]

So, when it comes to long-term survival and particularly innovation, organizations currently find themselves in a bit of a quandary. On one hand, they recognize that if they are to survive they must take risks and, on the other, they are petrified that if they take risks it could upset one or more of its stakeholders and certainly the status quo. They can't win. But win they must. Just look at the Eurofighter project. The fighter plane, which has been developed at a cost of billions, has been criticized as obsolete and technically flawed by Germany's Federal Audit Court. According to its report:[5]

- the plane is not permitted to take off when the air temperature drops below 5 degrees Celsius;

- the cockpit canopy may not withstand the impact of a bird flying into it;

- the speed is 300 mph less than required;

- the operational ceiling is 36,000 feet instead of 54,000 feet as planned;

- there are problems with electronic systems failures;

- the radar tracking system can show planes and missiles moving away when they are, in fact, attacking;

- the plane will cost 50 per cent more to operate than the Tornado; and

- development costs are rising from the current £4.3 billion.

But, as with any innovation of such a sophisticated nature, there are always problems that have to be overcome.

So, can such enterprises look towards a risk-free future? Let's find out in the final chapter.

Notes

1   Von Stamm, B. (2003) *The Innovation Wave: Meeting the Corporate Challenge*, Chichester: John Wiley & Sons, p. 9.

2   Buckley, N. (2003) 'Kraft cuts pack sizes to avert obesity lawsuits', *Financial Times*, 2 July, p. 21.

3   Witzel, M. (2002) *Builders and Dreamers: The Making and Meaning of Management*, London: Financial Times Prentice Hall, p. 269.

4   London, S. (2003) 'Why disruption can be good for business', *Financial Times*, 3 October, p. 14.

5   Sparks, J. (2003) 'Watchdog denounces "flawed" Eurofighter as unfit for combat', *Sunday Times*, 21 September, p. 7.

9 Looking Forward to a Risk-free Future?

Managing the multitude of risks we face can seem somewhat daunting and it appears that, irrespective of what we do to reduce the risks to humankind, there are those who believe that the our fate is pretty much sealed. As the quote above indicates, Martin Rees believes that we have no more than a 50:50 chance of surviving into the twenty-second century. Pretty depressing, but quite probable. Others believe that machines in the form of nanobots or robots will take over or that a comet will hit and destroy life on Earth. If we don't end up killing ourselves, maybe the computers will. Films such as *The Matrix* and *Terminator* paint a gloomy picture of our future, which may keep us on the edge of our seats now, but how would we feel if science fiction became science fact?

The Sunday Times compiled the following list of the nine terrible things that might happen to us over the coming century and, looking down the list, many are out of our control. So, perhaps we should all just give up and seek a hedonistic future or take to heart the words that adorn the front cover of *The Hitchhiker's Guide to the Galaxy* – 'Don't Panic'.

1   *The experiment that backfires.* This relates to the possibility of a particle collider creating a tiny black hole that would slowly suck all of Earth's matter into it. There is also the chance that it could create another Big Bang, which would destroy the universe.

2   *Machines take over.* The continued advance of technology and especially computers will eventually consume human life. We will become at one with the machines and we will become servants to super-intelligent androids.

3   *Nanobots.* Another variant of the 'technology takes over the future' scenario. Nanotechnology ('nano-' means very small, i.e. one thousand-millionth) is currently a hot area of research. Scientists hope to create nanobots that can maintain our bodies, create tiny machines and produce useful materials for humankind. They could also build themselves, which would be difficult to control. Such self-replication could lead to nanobots covering the Earth, creating some kind of grey soup.

4   *Bugs.* The rise of the super-bug is a well-known problem that is causing concern in medical circles. Such super-bugs have such a powerful ability to mutate that over time many have become re-

sistant to all but the most powerful antibiotics. Unless they are held in check, diseases such as AIDS, Ebola and, most recently, SARS have the capability of destroying great tranches of the human race. And even those diseases we thought we had eradicated, particularly in the West, are making a strong comeback. These include tuberculosis, cholera, malaria and even the bubonic plague. And we should not forget influenza, which has the capacity to kill tens of millions of people in a matter of months, as it did in 1919. With global temperatures rising, we may have to become accustomed to the diseases we more readily associate with exotic climates.

5   *Volcanoes.* The last time a large volcano, the size of which might worry us, erupted was almost 74,000 years ago. And erupt it did. The volcano in Sumatra created a 60-mile hole in the Earth's crust and encased the world in darkness for years. It also ejected some 1440 cubic miles of ash. A similar super eruption could have the capability of eliminating humankind. Other volcanic eruptions, smaller in size but equally capable of wreaking immense damage, are more likely to occur. Such major eruptions can lead to the plunging of large amounts of landmass into the oceans, leading to tidal waves that can devastate shore-based populations within hours.

6   *Earthquakes.* In a similar way, earthquakes pose a major threat to the world's population. Some of the most populous places on Earth sit on the top of major fault-lines. Take Tokyo, which sits at the junction of three tectonic plates, and San Francisco, situated on the San Andreas Fault. Both are long overdue a major event and the impacts will go beyond just the human. The likely disruption to the global finance community could prove to be catastrophic. It is clear that natural disasters rarely play out in isolation. As we have seen, risk is increasingly systemic.

7   *Meteorites. Deep Impact* may have been a great film, but the effect of a medium-to-large meteor could be significant. Size matters. Anything over 100 metres across can wipe out cities. And once you get to 1 kilometre across, the damage can go global. The rule of the dinosaurs was cut short by a meteor approximately 10 kilometres across. As yet we do not know the scale of the risks we face, but it is more likely that we will be killed by a deep impact than win the lottery.

8   *Heat.* The impacts of global warming (irrespective of whether it is a manmade phenomenon) cannot be overstated. Our weather systems are changing as the globe adapts to the changes in surface temperature. The result will be an increasing number of droughts, severe storms, and an increase in sea levels, which will threaten to engulf many of our major cities. The number of droughts has doubled over the last four years alone. The obvious danger we face is a runaway greenhouse effect that could heat up the Earth to the point where none of us can survive. That said, for those that believe the world is self-regulating, we may find that Mother Earth comes to our rescue.

9   *War.* Humans are natural born killers and warmongers. We have managed to claw ourselves out of the primordial soup to become what we are today. Conflict and the desire to fight are in our blood. Over the past few hundred years the sophistication of the weaponry at our disposal has grown considerably. The ability to destroy ourselves many times over has never been simpler and, despite the attempts by the US to hold despotic regimes in check, it seems that every country wants to 'go nuclear'.

All of this makes sorry and depressing reading, but we ought to get a grip and look to those risks that we can control rather than those that we can't. There is little value in burying our heads in the sand and waiting for the inevitable. But, by the same token, it is also naive to believe that we will face a risk-free future, as everything points to an increase, not a decrease, in either the complexity of risk or its impacts. We therefore have to become smarter at understanding and managing the risks that we face. So, here are ten steps to successful risk management.

1   Understand your risk appetite

Understanding what risks the organization is willing to take helps to define the boundary between acceptable and unacceptable risks. The level of risk taking should feed into the strategic intent of the organization and, more importantly, frame how the organization intends to manage them. Organizations should ask themselves the following questions in order to understand their risk appetite:

- What risks is the organization prepared to take in pursuit of its business goals and where is the boundary between these and those risks it is unwilling to take?

- Are the risks consistent with the organization's strategy?

- Where should exposure to risk be reduced?

- Is the organization too risk adverse and, as a result, missing opportunities?

- How will the organization's stakeholders be affected by the risks being taken?

In answering these five questions, the organization will know those risks it is willing to take, understand that some risks are necessary if it is to succeed in its allotted market, know how it intends to manage the risks it wishes to take, and how to avoid those it doesn't. These questions should also be applied to the individual functions, as this will ensure that the risks are known throughout the whole organization and, more importantly, it will help to create a healthy risk management culture.

2   Formalize the process

Relying on instinct, gut feeling or raw judgement is never the best way to manage risk. The inherent danger of relying on this type of approach is that things will be missed, information will not be captured or shared and risks will be either managed badly or not managed at all. This makes risk management a lottery and can lead to very nasty surprises. And we have all seen how extreme the consequences of poor risk management can be from the financial disaster at Barings Bank, the bursting of the dotcom bubble and the oil crisis of 1973. Formalizing the process of risk management ensures that everyone is aware of the dangers that lurk within their business and what is to be done about them. The process should be documented and actively managed by the appointment of risk officers throughout the enterprise, and by ensuring that the identification, management and reporting of risk is part of everyone's objectives.

Formalizing the process also ensures that the organization is able to prioritize its risk management actions by focusing on those risks that have the largest impact and highest probability. Furthermore, it means that the difference between the cost of managing a risk and its asso-

Smart quotes

Sarbanes-Oxley unleashed batteries of lawyers across the country. The result is a huge preoccupation with the dangers and risks of making the slightest mistake, as opposed to a reasonable approach to legitimate business risk.

William Donaldson

ciated financial impact on the firm if it materializes is appropriately balanced. And remember it is not just about process, as governance mechanisms also have a vital part to play, as does internal audit, which for many organizations is *the* risk manager.

3 Identify and categorize risks at all levels

Risk occurs at all levels in the organization – strategically, within major projects and programmes, and operationally. Increasingly, the source and nature of risk is becoming more diverse. Factors such as globalization, the Internet and rapid technological change have all served to introduce new risks that have to be managed. Formalizing the process ensures that risks are identified. But in order to manage them effectively, it is essential that they are appropriately categorized so that they are dealt with at the correct level within the organization and that suitably qualified personnel are involved with their management.

Chapter 2 should have given you more than enough of a head start to allow you to categorize those risks that are likely to impact your business. Using these to establish the basis of an enterprise risk management framework that suits your organization is one way in which to become more successful at managing risk.

4 Manage risks actively

Many organizations believe, quite wrongly, that the process of risk management stops at capturing and categorizing the risks. Such organizations also believe that risk management is a passive, not an active, process. The biggest problem in adopting the passive stance is that it leads to surprises and forces the organization to fight fires and manage crises. Such fire-fighting is a chronic waste of organizational resource and can do untold damage on a corporation's reputation. It is, unfortunately, well rewarded and considered a key skill in most circles. Active risk management involves continuously scanning the internal and external horizons for potential risks, taking time to understand what they might mean for the organization and taking positive decisions as to whether they will be managed or not. Although perhaps less exciting than fire-fighting, such an approach not only allows organizations to manage risk more effectively, but it also allows them to spot opportunities more readily. And it is the ability to spot opportunities and manage the risks associated with them that differentiates the market leaders from their competitors.

5   Develop a risk culture

Creating a culture that accepts and embraces risk is essential to being effective at risk management. The increasing complexity of the business environment necessitates a more mature approach to managing risk. Organizations can no longer afford to maintain a culture that blames, ignores or sanitizes failure, as this prevents risks from being spotted in the first place, let alone managed and reported on. Creating a no-surprise culture means allowing everyone to raise concerns and issues as they go about their daily work. Sanctioning those that highlight risks or those that fail only helps to push risk management off the agenda and promote a culture of self-preservation. In the long run this stifles innovation and results in a culture where no one is willing to take risk. We should, of course, never forget human behaviour, which can scupper even the most well-honed risk culture. Once you have

Smart quotes

The benefits of risk-taking are clear. Progress – economic or otherwise – implies risk-taking of some kind, to mark a break from convention and change for the better. Not only are there tangible rewards at the end of the process that may come from experimentation and the creation of new products, organizations also benefit from the confidence and experience acquired in the process.

Chris Frost, David Allen, James Porter, Philip Bloodworth

established an effective risk culture, guard it and nurture it because it will serve you well. Organizations that create a culture that embraces risk and recognizes the importance of coming clean when mistakes are made (see below) will be more successful than those that don't.

6 Learn from mistakes (yours and other people's)

> Even a mistake may turn out to be the one thing necessary to a worthwhile achievement.
>
> Henry Ford

Learning and adaptation are two of the many things that set us aside from the rest of the animal kingdom. They are also essential components of our own personal development and advancement. Apart from learning in the formal setting of school, or the training room, we learn from mistakes and success. Unfortunately, because mistakes and failure have negative connotations we do not learn enough from them. We would rather brush them under the carpet and pretend they never happened. Similarly, success breeds hubris, which can also prevent us from learning as much we could. For the majority of us, the management and avoidance of risk could be vastly improved if only we would take more care in the way we learn from success and failure. There are enough lessons out there, if only we would seek them out. For many, though, it's a case of history repeating itself.

7 Ask yourself difficult questions

At regular intervals it is a good idea for organizations to ask themselves, 'What could happen in the future that would put the business at risk?'

In asking this question it is essential to focus on all aspects of the risk continuum, from the strategic level right through to the operational. Asking this question offers two distinct advantages. First, it ensures that risk is kept at the forefront of the board's and every functional head's mind. Second, it ensures that the risks that the organization faces are kept current. Being able to think the unthinkable and challenge the status quo is difficult but in doing so it helps to keep the business agile and fighting fit. This is why Shell was able to ride out the 1970s oil crisis and why GE under the direction of Jack Welch was able to maintain a dominant market position for so long.

> The greatest mistake you can make in life is to be continually fearing you will make one.
>
> Elbert Hubbard

8 Use known methods and tools to support you

Effective risk management relies on the discipline of capturing information, tracking the management of risks once identified and regularly reporting on their status (i.e. their impact, probability and actions associated with their management). Rather than reinventing the wheel, it is far better to use tried and tested methods and tools to support you. And, because there are so many vendors selling risk management tools, methods and services, there is normally a tool to manage the various kinds of risks the organization faces, be they financial, operational, technical or more general in nature. Methods and tools will never replace the need for judgement and effective decision making, so never expect a tool to replace the need for human intervention. Always remember the adage – *A fool with a tool is still a fool.*

9 Use expert advice where required

Managing risk is not an easy task and sometimes it is necessary to seek professional help. Risk management professionals and specialists can provide advice on the general aspects of risk management, including process, risk factors and mitigation strategies, as well as detailed knowledge and advice on specific categories of risk. Although the use of internal auditors is good for assessing controls and generic risks, this approach often lacks the specialist skills of the external expert. Internal auditors can also lack the creativity required to manage risk, as well as the ability to see the upside of risk – opportunity.

Seeking professional help not only improves the risk management process, but it also allows the organization to begin to develop a wider capability in risk management through the effective transfer of knowledge. The other advantage of employing external experts is that they can challenge the status quo and the key decision makers much more effectively, principally because they do not have to work there.

10   Remember to balance risk with reward

Managing risk is not all about looking for problems. Ultimately it is about maintaining a balance between risk and reward. The ability to make profits depends on making appropriate decisions, having first assessed the level of return from the investment and the risks it might present. Where these are out of balance, it will result in either a crash-and-burn scenario, as we saw with the dotcoms, or a slow growth that allows you to become a target for takeover. Balancing risk with opportunity is key because it allows you to push the boundaries of the organization while at the same time not betting the company on unnecessary or rash ventures.

Smart people to have on your side: Dietrich Dörner

Dörner is Professor of Psychology at the University of Bamberg and a recognized authority on cognitive behaviour.

In *The Logic of Failure*, Dörner states that our inability to spot failures-in-the-making stems from the way we have developed a tendency to deal with problems on an ad hoc basis, rather than looking at them more widely and systemically.

Risk will always be with us and, in order to be effective at risk management, we must learn to manage it to the best of our abilities. Who needs a risk-free future anyway? Life would be too dull!

Smart quotes

There was a very cautious man,
Who never laughed or cried.
He never risked, he never lost,
He never won nor tried.
And when one day he passed away,
His insurance was denied,
For since he never really lived,
They claimed he never died!

Dennis Waitley

Glossary

What follows is a glossary containing the common terms and concepts associated with risk and risk management.

A-Score

A method for assessing whether a company is A-OK. Developed by John Argenti, the A-Score can predict an impending crisis nine times out of ten. The A-Score identifies 10 defects, 3 mistakes and 4 symptoms of a failing organization.

ACID

This acronym refers to electronic transactions, which, if they are to be trusted, should be:

- **A**tomic – the transaction cannot be split into its component parts and will either fail completely or succeed completely.

- **C**onsistent – a transaction is said to be consistent if all parties involved agree on the critical facts of the exchange.

- **I**solated – transactions do not interfere with each other.

- **D**urable – when a failure occurs the transaction can be recovered to its last consistent state.

ACID transactions are robust because they are unaffected by failures of any kind (human, network and/or hardware).

Basle Accord

The 1988 Basle Accord (also known as the Bank for International Standards Accord) was designed to establish a set of international guidelines that linked a bank's credit exposure to its minimum capital requirement. Although initially focused on credit risk, subsequent amendments have extended this to market risk and risk-based capital requirements.

Business continuity planning

Interest in business continuity planning has grown considerably since the corporate world was shocked into preparing for the worst with the turning of the millennium. Although 2000 came and went without any great disasters, the heightened awareness of business continuity planning remained. Although often assumed to be about maintaining business operations following a natural disaster, such as an earthquake, it should be noted that the majority of disasters are caused by power outages and fire. According to James Barnes, author of *A Guide to Business Continuity Planning*, there are at least 75 known causes for a disaster condition ranging from the very serious, such as volcanoes and hurricanes, to the minor, such as insect infestation.

The process of creating business continuity plans usually follows five steps:[1]

- Establishing the project that develops the business continuity plan. This involves the standard project management activities associated with setting up any project.

- Assessing the internal and external threats to the business. This involves assessing the criticality of business processes and systems along with their resource requirements and determining the recovery time for each.

- Selecting an appropriate strategy to enhance the survivability of the critical components of the business. This is really about managing the risk by reducing their likelihood or impact.

- Developing the business continuity plan. The purpose of the plan is to recreate the critical business components should they fail. This is all about re-establishing normal business activity as soon as possible after a disaster strikes.

- Testing and maintaining the plan, once developed.

Capital asset pricing model (CAPM)

A theoretical framework comparing risk and return on shares. According to the model, financial markets will compensate investors for taking market risk, but not on specific risk (which can be diversified).

Chief risk officer

An executive role, sometimes at board level, that is responsible for the management of an enterprise's risk.

Collatorized debt obligations (CDO)

Securities backed by pools of bonds or loans. Their purpose is to reduce an investor's exposure to an individual bond or loan by pooling a variety of credits, typically junk bonds, and using the cashflow to back securities with different risk ratings.

Country risk

Country risk is the risk that a counterpart will not be able to pay its obligations because of cross-border restrictions on the availability of a given currency. Where the country's economy is weak, or their political situation poor, their risk rating tends to be high.

Credit rating

Every company issuing debt is rated according to its creditworthiness by two major agencies (see *Risk-rating agencies*). The rating is based on a combination of the default risk and the likelihood of payment for the issuer.

- For those organizations that are believed to be capable of meeting their financial obligations their credit ratings range from AAA through AA to A. This means that the organization concerned has a low credit risk.

- For those organizations that are more vulnerable to changes in economic or market conditions and are therefore more likely to find it difficult (or unwilling) to meet their financial obligations, their credit ratings range from BBB+/BBB through BBB- and BB+/BB to BB- (the plus and minus sign indicates the relative position within the ratings and is an important differentiator).

- For those organizations that are the most vulnerable to non-payment and are particularly exposed to adverse economic and market conditions their rating ranges from CCC through CC to C. Such organizations have the highest credit risk.

Those organizations with a rating of AAA, AA, A and BBB are considered to be of investment grade. Those rated lower are not investment grade and are considered to be more risky and speculative.

Credit risk

The risk associated with the ability (or willingness) of a third party to repay money owed. The creditworthiness of an organization determines the interest rate paid on the loan and the amount of collateral required to secure the loan in the first place.

Currency exchange risk

The risk associated with the value of foreign currency holdings caused by fluctuations in the currency markets.

Decision trees

A technique for determining the potential outcomes of a course of action, and hence risk, as an aid to decision making.

Delphi process

The Delphi process is a forecasting technique that is based on the repetitive polling of experts. The process involves seeking the opinion of a group of experts on a particular subject, such as the closing value of the Dow–Jones index on 31 December. Once the experts have made their forecast the results are shared anonymously across the group.

Each can then modify his or her forecast in light of the group results. The process continues until the results stabilize.

Derivatives

A derivative is a financial instrument that derives its value from the value of other instruments.

Diversification

A risk management strategy that involves investing in different market sectors and countries as a means of reducing exposure to market risk.

Environment risk

The risk that the environment (be it the global climate, local river courses, the food chain etc.) is damaged as a direct consequence of industrial and business activity.

Fraud detection technologies[2]

Online merchants have a number of fraud detection technologies available to them with which to manage the risks of online theft. If used in combination they can be quite effective.

- Address verification systems. These validate the billing address provided by the purchaser against the billing address information held by the card issuer.

- Card verification methods. This consists of a 3–4-digit code that is printed but not embossed on the card, or contained within the magnetic strip. The online merchant can request the number as an additional security measure. Should the card be counterfeit it will not contain this number.

- Lockout mechanisms. These are specifically designed to prevent randomly generated credit card numbers from being used by fraudsters. The usual traits of a randomly generated card attack include multiple transactions with similar card numbers, a large number of declined transactions and the failure of the address verification test.

- Negative lists. These hold information that can be used by the online merchant to assess the level of risk a transaction might represent. For example, the lists hold information about charge-backs against particular card numbers, odd billing addresses and known countries where fraud is rife, such as Nigeria and Eastern Europe.

- Fraud rules. These are designed to pinpoint high-risk transactions using a rules-based selection process. The rules can vary and are often designed by the online merchant. Examples include purchases over a certain amount, multiple purchases of a single item and so on.

- Risk scoring. This involves the use of risk-scoring tools based on statistical models of fraudulent transactions and it is probably the most effective detection mechanism available to online merchants.

Hedging

Hedging is a way of dealing with unwanted risks. It involves acquiring a new risk that completely offsets the unwanted risk. The net effect of this is zero, resulting in no loss or gain. However, it is rare to find a completely safe hedge, as they usually cost something, and in some cases they can go disastrously wrong, as with Long-Term Capital Management in 1998 (see Chapter 2). The primary financial instruments for hedging are:

- Forwards – an agreement to buy or sell shares in a company, foreign exchange or commodities at an agreed rate at a specified point in the future. The buyer in the deal is said to be taking the long position and the seller the short position. The specified point in the future when the deal is executed is the maturity date and the agreed price the delivery price.

- Swaps – an agreement between two parties to exchange each other's commitments at an agreed rate at a specified point in the future. Swaps are usually associated with interest rates and currencies. Swaps have been around since the 1920s but have only been popular within the financial markets since the 1980s. Interest rate swaps are where two parties agree to meet each other's interest rate payments when they become due. Currency swaps are more complex because it can be difficult to cover the risk entirely due to variations in currency values. As a result, it is usual for a swap to consist of two or more agreements.

- Options – these give someone the right (not the obligation) to buy or sell shares, currency and commodities at an agreed price at a specified point in the future. The key distinction here is that, unlike swaps and forwards, the buyer does not have to purchase should market conditions be more favourable. The price at which the shares, currency or commodities can be purchased is known as the exercise price, and taking up the right is known as exercising. The date at which the option is (or is not) exercised is called the expiration date.

Interest rate risk

The risk associated with the value of fixed income obligations changing as a result of more favourable terms being available on the open market.

Internal audit

An organizational function which involves the assessment, identification and monitoring of the major risks that face an enterprise.

Liquidity risk

Probably the most important and least understood risk. It relates to the ability (or inability) to buy or sell something at short notice at a fair or good rate. Liquidity risk is usually the result of buyers not being found fast enough. From a purely market perspective, liquidity risk occurs when markets do not perform in a perfect way. When there is a danger of a global lack of liquidity, such as at the turn of the millennium, central banks can take deliberate steps to ensure markets remain liquid in times of crisis.

Monte Carlo simulation

Named after the roulette wheels in Monte Carlo, which are considered to be mechanisms for generating random numbers.

Operational risk

Risks caused by losses associated with mistakes, failure of information systems, deliberate sabotage by staff, poor internal controls and disasters (such as flooding, hurricanes and so on). Operational risks are more vague than the other forms of risk and require more effort to define. However, failure to manage them can lead to significant financial loss.

Opportunity cost

The cost of not doing something else, where the returns on investment might be higher.

Personal risk

Risks that we face as individuals, typically outside the workplace. These include those related to our health, personal finance and retirement. They also extend to how we maintain our employability.

Probability

The chance that something could happen. When expressed as a number, probability can range from 0 (the event is impossible and will never occur) to 1 (the event will happen; it is certain to occur).

Programme and project risk

The risk associated with the failure of a major project or programme. Because most change in organizations is now stepwise rather than incremental, the importance of projects and programmes has increased significantly, as have the risks associated with their failure.

Reputational risk

The risk that the reputation of an individual or organization is irreparably damaged as a result of a disaster, product failure, illegal actions etc. This also extends to the impact of third parties on the reputation of a company or individual.

Risk culture

According to John Holiwell,[3] the risk culture in an organization is a critical factor in the management of risk. Creating an appropriate risk culture means three things:

- Understanding the board's appetite for risk. This is important as it dictates how much risk the organization is prepared to take.

- Being honest. There is little point in taking risks if the consequences of taking them are hidden from view or, when they are raised, are ignored. Being honest means having open discussions and being willing to take the necessary actions to manage risk.

- Ensuring risk management is understood throughout the organization.

Risk framework

A way of capturing and then describing the types of risk the enterprise is likely to face. This normally identifies, in broad terms, the nature and sources of its primary risks and will include internal as well as external sources.

Risk governance

Management committees responsible for overseeing and monitoring the management of risk. These typically include strategic and business risk, credit risk, project and programme risk.

Risk management – general process

The process through which risks are identified, managed and controlled. Risk management involves a continuous process that has four basic steps:

- identification

- quantification

- response development

- monitor and control.

Risk management – banking

The approach to risk management within the banking community differs quite considerably from the process described above. Risk management in banking usually involves:

- Setting global target earnings and risk limits.

- Translating the goals into business unit target revenues, risk limits and guidelines.

- Establishing processes for the monitoring and reporting of risks at the transaction as well as the consolidated level. The aggregated figures are used to manage the bank's overall risk.

Risk management – operational

According to the Risk Management Association, effective operational risk management requires organizations to establish a framework that consists of a set of integrated processes, tools and mitigation strategies. Such a framework has six components to it:

- strategy

- risk policies

- risk management process

- risk mitigation

- operations management

- culture

Risk-rating agencies

The two most widely accepted credit risk-rating agencies are Moody and Standard & Poor. Both are considered to have the necessary expertise in credit rating and are believed to be unbiased evaluators of an organization's ability to meet its financial obligations. The rating process involves assessing:

- Qualitative factors such as the capability of management, the vulnerability of the organization to external change and threats, such as regulation, technology and competition, as well as its growth potential and industrial relations track record.

- Quantitative factors as contained within an organization's financial accounts.

The rating process culminates in the issuing of a credit rating (see *Credit rating*), which determines the terms under which the organization can issue debt. Ratings are usually reviewed once a year, taking into account new financial reports and other factors. Because things can change very rapidly with the financial position of an organization, corporations can be subject to a credit watch notice that indicates the rating is likely to change. In most cases this results in a reduction in the credit rating.

Risk register

A document that summarizes risk. The register typically includes:

- a description of the risk;

- the risk's scenario for maturity;

- the impact should it mature;

- the probability or likelihood of it maturing;

- the priority score (the product of the impact and probability);

- the management strategy that describes how the risk will be addressed; and

- the containment strategy, which describes what will happen if the risk matures.

Scenario planning

A scenario is a tool for describing, assessing and understanding possible futures. The process of scenario planning originated in the oil company Shell and was used to navigate them through the oil crisis of the 1970s. Scenario planning is an important tool for managing strategic risk, as it allows organizations to think outside the box and consider their future more thoroughly. The process of developing and assessing scenarios usually follows the steps below:

- The existing mental models associated with the organization are captured and challenged as a way of preparing the organization's leaders to revisit their assumptions and open their minds.

- The business context is assessed by taking into consideration political, social, technological and environmental drivers. These are prioritized according to their importance to the organization.

- The drivers are then used to construct three or four scenarios (essentially narratives describing the future), which are used by the organization to asses their implications and develop strategies that work, irrespective of which scenario unfolds.

- The final step is the identification of the leading indicators of each scenario. These will be tracked by the organization as a means of assessing which scenario, or combination of scenarios, is actually unfolding. The indicators are also used to trigger specific actions as defined in the strategy.

The real advantage of scenario planning is that it allows organizations to adapt more quickly to what is happening around them and to anticipate their future more effectively.

Sensitivity analysis

Sensitivity analysis is a method of identifying key variables underlying a financial forecast or investment project and assessing the impact of any change in these variables on cashflow and profitability. The analysis involves shifting the value of one variable at a time and seeing the impact on the financial forecast or project. To assist this process it is necessary to ask 'what if' questions such as: What if the global market went into recession? What if interest rates had to rise 5 per cent? What if the fixed price for a product went up by 10 per cent? The results of the sensitivity analysis feed into the risk identification process.

Settlement risk

The risk that a transaction fails at the time of settlement.

Strategic risk

The risk that the company could fail, be subject to a takeover bid or suffer major financial consequences as a direct result of a flawed strategy, either in terms of the strategy itself, or in the way it has been executed.

Swaps

Interest rate swaps have been a popular tool for managing risks since the 1980s. They exist because of the differences in interest rates, currency values and credit ratings of the institutions involved with executing the swap. If, for example, company A has a good credit rating in market X but a poor one in market Y, and company B has a good rating in market Y but a poor one in market X, there is an opportunity to execute a swap. In this instance, company A would borrow money on behalf of company B to allow it to operate in market Y and company B would borrow money on behalf of company A to allow it to operate in market X. This allows both companies to operate with a reduced risk in their secondary markets.

The two forms of swaps are:

- Interest rate swaps, where the two parties agree to pay the other's interest rate payments when they become due. The swap does not apply to the loan itself, only the interest.

- Currency swaps, which involves raising a loan in one currency and then swapping it into another at an agreed exchange rate. Debt is serviced in the same way as an interest rate swap, and once the maturity date has been reached, the loan amount will be re-exchanged at a pre-agreed rate.

Talent risk

The risk associated with the loss of productive and effective employees, as well as those who are considered to have a future in the firm.

Technology risk

According to Lewis Branscomb and Philip Auerwald, authors of *Taking Technical Risks*, risk falls into three categories:

- Technical risk. This is associated with the problems that can occur during the development and application of any new or emerging technology. Issues such as safety, security, reliability and applicability are all relevant.

- The availability of competencies and complementary technologies required to support the introduction of a new technology. This is typically associated with the skills required to implement the new technology, and it is most commonly found within IT projects. There are three main risks to manage under this category:

  1 Ignorance of prevailing knowledge. Technicians may not be aware of the full extent of the new technology or the techniques used to implement it, even though the organization expects them to understand all aspects of it. With faster cycle times, and shortening project horizons, there is often no time to gain the necessary understanding prior to attempting its implementation; the project becomes the training ground, and very often a disaster.

  2 Failure to use prevailing knowledge. Although aware of current tools, techniques and technologies, organizational pressure for rapid implementation often means there is no opportunity to use them. Such time pressure means there is little time to train staff, which in turn reduces the chances of implementing the new technology successfully. This has a subsequent knock-on effect in achieving the benefits from the investment.

  3 Conditions beyond prevailing knowledge. This is the classic leading edge technology that involves pioneering activity and trailblazing by the experts, using hitherto untried and untested technologies, tools or techniques.

- Specification achieveability. This is associated with the outcome of the technology implementation in terms of its ability to meet the original specification. All too often the requirements, both in terms of functionality and performance, are not met. Once again this will affect the business case, the benefits, and the long-term value of the product if it is to be sold on the open market.

Value at risk (VaR)[4]

Value at risk is defined as the worst loss that might be expected from holding a security or portfolio over a given period of time and given a specified level of probability. The strict definition is 'the maximum loss over a given period such that there is a 1 per cent probability that the actual loss over the given period will be larger'. VaR does not state the full extent of the loss, it merely indicates how likely the loss will exceed the VaR figure. Calculating the VaR involves:

- Deriving the forward distribution of the portfolio (or the return on the portfolio at a given point in the future). This distribution is either assumed to follow a normal distribution (parametric VaR) or derived from historical data (non-parametric VaR).

- Calculating the first percentile of the forward distribution.

- VaR is the maximum loss at the 99 per cent confidence level relative to the expected value of the portfolio at the target horizon.

VaR not only provides a consistent approach to managing risks across an institution but also ensures risks are visible rather than hidden from view. In addition, it doubles up as a senior management-reporting tool and is an important consideration when deriving credit ratings.

Volatility

One of the basic statistical measures of risk. The volatility of an investment portfolio is directly related to how far its value varies from the mean. There are two methods for measuring the volatility in financial markets. The first is to use historical data about the investment. Although useful as a way of establishing trends, it can never be fully relied upon because the level of volatility will depend on the period over which the data is gathered. The second is to use models, such as Black-Scholes, to estimate the volatility.

Z-Score

The Z-Score was developed by Edward Altman, Professor of Finance at New York University School of Business. The Z-Score is based on five weighted financial ratios and indicates whether a company is heading for insolvency. A score of less than 1.8 usually indicates a failure in the making, as it did for the four years running up to the failure of Enron.

Notes

1   Barnes, J.C. (2001) *A Guide to Business Continuity Planning*, Chichester: John Wiley & Sons, p. 19.

2   For more detail see, ClearCommerce White Paper, *Fraud Prevention Guide*.

3   Holiwell, J. (1998) 'Risk: enough rope to hang the business?' in *Mastering Finance: The definitive guide to the foundations and frontiers of finance*, London: Financial Times Pitman Publishing, pp. 293–7.

4   Crouhy, M., Galai D. and Mark D. (2001) *Risk Management*, New York: McGraw-Hill, pp. 187–92.

Index